Important: Please read this page before using the dBASE III Plus program, a copy of which is being made available to you for use in conjunction with this Textbook pursuant to the terms of this Agreement for educational, training and/or demonstration purposes. By using the dBASE III PLUS program, you show your agreement to the terms of this license.

EXCLUSIONS OF WARRANTIES AND LIMITATIONS OF LIABILITY

THE COPY OF THE dBASE III PLUS PROGRAM MADE AVAILABLE FOR USE WITH THIS TEXTBOOK IS A LIMITED FUNCTIONALITY VERSION OF dBASE III PLUS, AND IS INTENDED SOLELY FOR EDUCATIONAL, TRAINING AND DEMONSTRATION PURPOSES. ACCORDINGLY, THIS COPY OF dBASE III PLUS IS PROVIDED "AS IS," WITHOUT WARRANTY OF ANY KIND FROM ASHTON-TATE OR HOLT RINEHART & WINSTON. ASHTON-TATE AND HOLT RINEHART & WINSTON HEREBY DISCLAIM ALL WARRANTIES OF ANY KIND WITH RESPECT TO THIS LIMITED FUNCTIONALITY COPY OF dBASE III PLUS, INCLUDING WITHOUT LIMITATION THE IMPLIED WARRANTIES OF MERCHANTABILITY AND FITNESS FOR A PARTICULAR PURPOSE. NEITHER ASHTON-TATE NOR HOLT RINEHART & WINSTON SHALL BE LIABLE UNDER ANY CIRCUMSTANCES FOR CONSEQUENTIAL, INCIDENTAL, SPECIAL OR EXEMPLARY DAMAGES ARISING OUT OF THE USE OF THIS LIMITED FUNCTIONALITY COPY OF dBASE III PLUS, EVEN IF ASHTON-TATE OR HOLT RINEHART & WINSTON HAS BEEN APPRISED OF THE LIKELIHOOD OF SUCH DAMAGES OCCURRING. IN NO EVENT WILL ASHTON-TATE'S OR HOLT RINEHART & WINSTON'S LIABILITY (WHETHER BASED ON AN ACTION OR CLAIM IN CONTRACT, TORT OR OTHERWISE) ARISING OUT OF THE USE OF THIS LIMITED FUNCTIONALITY COPY OF dBASE III PLUS EXCEED THE AMOUNT PAID FOR THIS TEXTBOOK.

LIMITED USE SOFTWARE LICENSE AGREEMENT

DEFINITIONS

The term "Software" as used in this agreement means the Limited Use version of dBASE III PLUS which is made available for use in conjunction with this Textbook solely for educational, training and/or demonstration purposes. The term "Software Copies" means the actual copies of all or any portion of the Software, including back-ups, updates, merged or partial copies permitted hereunder.

PERMITTED USES

You may:

- Load into RAM and use the Software on a single terminal or a single workstation of a computer (or its replacement).
- Install the Software onto a permanent storage device (a hard disk drive).
- Make and maintain up to three back up copies provided they are used only for back-up purposes, and you keep possession of the back-ups. In addition, all the information appearing on the original disk labels (including copyright notice) must be copied onto the back-up labels.

This license gives you certain limited rights to use the Software and Software Copies for educational, training and/or demonstration purposes. You do not become the owner of and Ashton-Tate retains title to, all the Software and Software Copies. In addition, you agree to use reasonable efforts to protect the Software from unauthorized use, reproduction, distribution or publication.

All rights not specifically granted in this license are reserved by Ashton-Tate.

USES NOT PERMITTED

You may not:

- Make copies of the Software, except as permitted above.
- Rent, lease, sublicense, time-share, lend or transfer the Software, Software Copies or your rights under this license except that transfers may be made with Ashton-Tate's prior written authorization.
- Alter, decompile, disassemble, or reverse-engineer the Software.
- Remove or obscure the Ashton-Tate copyright and trademark notices.
- Use the Software or Software Copies outside the United States or Canada.

DURATION

This agreement is effective from the day you first use the Software. Your license continues for fifty years or until you return to Ashton-Tate the original disks and any back-up copies, whichever comes first.

If you breach this agreement, Ashton-Tate can terminate this license upon notifying you in writing. You will be required to return all Software Copies. Ashton-Tate can also enforce our other legal rights.

GENERAL

This agreement represents the entire understanding and agreement regarding the Software and Software Copies and supersedes any prior purchase order, communication, advertising or representation.

This license may only be modified in a written amendment signed by an authorized Ashton-Tate officer. If any provision of this agreement shall be unlawful, void, or for any reason unenforceable, it shall be deemed severable from, and shall in no way affect the validity or enforceability of the remaining provisions of this agreement. This agreement will be governed by California law.

SECOND EDITION

PRODUCTIVITY SOFTWARE GUIDE

Featuring:
WordPerfect™
Lotus® 1-2-3 and
Joe Spreadsheet™
(a 1-2-3® Workalike)
dBASE III PLUS™

SECOND EDITION

PRODUCTIVITY SOFTWARE GUIDE

Featuring:
WordPerfect™
Lotus® 1-2-3 and
Joe Spreadsheet™
(a 1-2-3® Workalike)
dBASE III PLUS™

Charles S. Parker
The University of New Mexico, Albuquerque, New Mexico
The College of Santa Fe, Santa Fe, New Mexico

Janet R. Wilson
Seattle University, Seattle, Washington

THE DRYDEN PRESS
Chicago Fort Worth San Francisco
Philadelphia Montreal Toronto
London Sydney Tokyo

Acquisitions Editor: DeVilla Williams
Developmental Editor: Rita West
Project Editor: Karen Hill
Design Supervisor: Alan Wendt
Production Manager: Barb Bahnsen
Director of Editing, Design, and Production: Jane Perkins
Cover Designer: Stuart Paterson
Copy Editor: Maureen Duffy
Text Type: 12/13 Times Roman

Library of Congress Cataloging-in-Publication Data
Parker, Charles S., 1945–
Productivity software guide: featuring WordPerfect, Lotus 1-2-3 and Joe Spreadsheet (a 1-2-3 workalike), dBASE III Plus/Charles S. Parker, Janet Wilson. — 2nd ed.
p. cm.
ISBN 0-03-039637-9 (with software)
ISBN 0-03-047067-6 (without software)
1. Computer software. 2. WordPerfect (Computer program) 3. Lotus 1-2-3 (Computer program) 4. Joe Spreadsheet (Computer program) I. Wilson, Janet. II. Title
QA76.754.P36 1990
005.36—dc20 89-78194
CIP

Printed in the United States of America
012-021-987654321

Address orders:
The Dryden Press
Orlando, FL 32887

Address editorial correspondence:
The Dryden Press
908 N. Elm Street
Hinsdale, IL 60521

The Dryden Press
Holt, Rinehart and Winston
Saunders College Publishing

PREFACE

With the increase in the number of productivity software packages, such as word processors, spreadsheets, and database management systems, any person (from the clerical worker to the company president, or from the student to the professor) can effectively tap the power of computers.

Productivity Software Guide discusses the basics of four popular productivity software products: WordPerfect (a word processor), Lotus 1-2-3 and Joe Spreadsheet (two spreadsheet packages), and dBASE III PLUS (a database management system). These products are each the property of some software vendor and can only be legally used if an appropriate use license has been acquired from the vendor or authorized distributor. The Dryden Press—the publisher of this guide—has signed agreements that allow adopting institutions to use the educational versions of WordPerfect and dBASE III PLUS, as well as to use the full-featured version of Joe Spreadsheet (which looks and works a lot like 1-2-3).

The first section of the guide includes some background information relating to use of your microcomputer system. The following three sections cover the software programs (Joe Spreadsheet is covered in the section with 1-2-3). By progressing through each section and working through the exercises presented, the user will become familiar with many of the most commonly used functions of each program.

Users of this guide are assumed to be working on computer systems with either the PC-DOS or MS-DOS operating systems. The computer system should be equipped with at least 256K of main memory.

Acknowledgments

I wish to thank the following reviewers, who provided helpful comments and suggestions that have been incorporated in this manual: Edward G. Martin, Kingsborough Community College; Marilyn Moore, Purdue University; Susan Silvera, Los Angeles Trade-Technical College; Elias R. Callahan, Jr., Mississippi State University. I also wish to thank DeVilla Williams, Acquisitions Editor; Rita West, Developmental Editor; and the excellent staff at The Dryden Press for their guidance and support. Family and closest friends are to be thanked for their patience and encouragement.

Janet R. Wilson
Revised February 1990

TRADE NAMES

dBASE, dBASE II, dBASE III, and dBASE III PLUS are trademarks of Ashton-Tate.

WordPerfect is the trademark of WordPerfect Corporation.

Lotus, 1-2-3, and Symphony are trademarks of Lotus Development Corporation.

Joe and Joe Spreadsheet are trademarks of Holt, Rinehart and Winston, Inc. Copyright © 1987, 1986 by Goldstein Software, Inc. Distributed under license to Holt, Rinehart and Winston, Inc.

IBM PC, IBM PC XT, IBM PC AT, PS/2, and PC DOS are trademarks of International Business Machines Corporation.

MS-DOS is a trademark of Microsoft Corporation.

CONTENTS

INTERMEDIATE WORDPERFECT FUNCTIONS

ADVANCED WORDPERFECT FUNCTIONS

SECTION 3
SPREADSHEETS

BEGINNING SPREADSHEET FUNCTIONS

INTERMEDIATE SPREADSHEET FUNCTIONS

PRESENTATION GRAPHICS

SECTION 4
DATABASE

BEGINNING DATABASE FUNCTIONS

INTERMEDIATE DATABASE FUNCTIONS

ADVANCED DATABASE FUNCTIONS

SECTION I
THE OPERATING SYSTEM

PREVIEW

As you begin your interaction with the computer, you may be looking forward to all you will be able to accomplish with this powerful tool. You may also be asking yourself, Can I master the terminology and procedures? The answer to this question is YES.

Learning to operate a computer is a bit like learning to drive a car. When operating the car, you must first insert the key; you then follow a sequence of steps, such as: turn the key in a certain direction, wait for the car engine to start, change gears, press on the accelerator, and start driving. In other words, there is a sequence of steps that you follow when starting and driving the car that may seem second nature to you now, but that at one time may have caused you some apprehension. With time, you may have even learned to enjoy certain aspects of driving. It certainly makes your life more convenient. The car is a powerful tool, which does many things to improve the quality of our lives. The same principles are true when learning to operate a computer. It may cause some apprehension at first, but soon, such things as turning on the computer and creating documents with your favorite software program will become second nature, and the computer may become a valuable tool in your life.

When you drove a car for the first time, someone was probably in the car with you giving you step-by-step instructions. This guide is written to do the same type of thing by teaching you how to operate your computer in a step-by-step process. The guide is broken down into four main sections: Section I, an introduction to the operating system; Section II, how to use WordPerfect; Section III, how to use 1-2-3 or Joe Spreadsheet; and Section IV, how to use dBASE III Plus. Each of these sections pertains to a software program written by computer programmers. The programs were designed to save you a lot of work, and they take many months to design. The programs include instructions that allow certain steps to be completed when you press a combination of keys on the keyboard. In WordPerfect, for example, you can press a combination of the Shift key and the F7 key to reach a list of options for printing a document. By selecting a number corresponding to one of the options in the list, you can print a document. This is an easy sequence of steps and takes only a few seconds to complete; however, it may have taken many different instructions in the computer program to allow you to perform these few steps. In other words, you perform a simple sequence of steps to tell your software program what to do, but a program is a more detailed sequence of instructions that tell the computer what to do.

Before learning to use a software program, you should know something about the machine on which you are running the programs. It is always good to have some background information so that the operation is smooth and relatively free of problems.

EXERCISE 1.1. HOW TO IDENTIFY COMPUTER SYSTEM COMPONENTS

In general, a computer system contains many parts. Often the computer is thought of as one large electronic device, but, in fact, it contains both electronic and mechanical parts. The mechanical parts are similar to those in electric typewriters. Many computer parts are electronic, with impulses running through silicon chips, which are connected with wires. At any rate, the combination of electronic and mechanical parts makes up what is referred to as *hardware*. The parts of the hardware are called the central processing unit, keyboard, monitor, hard disk drive, diskette drive, and printer. These will be discussed shortly.

All of the electromechanical parts of the computer, however, are useless without the direction of a written program. These programs are called *software*. Some software programs are written and stored on chips within the computer hardware. *System software* contains instructions that coördinate the various parts of the computer system to make it run rapidly and efficiently. System software programs are the necessary component (much like the gasoline in an automobile) that allows the computer to operate. One of the most common types of system software programs used with IBM computers and IBM-compatible computers is PC- or MS-DOS. These programs are the operating system software programs and are critical to the supervision of the computer's work. Later in this section you will learn more about both of these operating systems.

Other software programs run on the hardware and tell the computer to perform a specific, job-related task. These types of programs are often called *application software*. The three programs discussed in this guide (WordPerfect, dBASE III Plus, and Joe Spreadsheet or Lotus 1-2-3) are examples of application software. Frequently, the application software program, such as WordPerfect, is contained on a diskette. This diskette is called the *program disk*.

Files are what you will use to organize and store the material you create with your application software programs. With WordPerfect, for example, each file will contain one or more specific documents that you have prepared, such as a letter, manuscript, or memorandum. With Lotus 1-2-3 or Joe Spreadsheet, files can contain budgets, asset amortization tables, and profit-and-loss statements. With dBASE III Plus, you can create files of such items as employee records, vendor records, or client records. These files are often stored on a blank disk usually called the *data disk*. You give each file a name to help you remember what it contains and to help you locate it among a group of files stored on the data disk.

The Hardware Components

All computer systems contain similar basic components. These are:

* a microprocessor (or processor)
* memory
* a monitor
* a keyboard
* a printer
* secondary storage

The Microprocessor

As mentioned earlier, many of the physical components of the computer are made up of silicon chips and wires. If you looked inside your computer, you would see primarily a mass of wires and chips. Much of this area is the *central processing unit,* or *CPU,* and the *memory*. Both the CPU and memory are contained on silicon chips. The CPU is often referred to as the "brain" of the computer system. This is a good analogy, because the CPU literally controls the very functions of the system and coordinates its activities—transmitting and receiving data through electrical impulses.

Memory

A microcomputer system has two kinds of memory chips—*ROM* and *RAM*. These memory components are also contained on silicon chips. ROM stands for *read-only memory* and contains programs that are installed by the manufacturer. ROM generally can be read (the information can be used by the computer) but cannot be written to (data cannot be stored over it). These program instructions are necessary for many of the functions of the computer. RAM stands for *random access memory* chips. RAM temporarily holds all program instructions and data used by the CPU. An application program such as WordPerfect is temporarily stored in RAM as are the data from documents on which you are working.

The Monitor

The monitor resembles a TV screen. It is the screen on which you can see your document as you type in WordPerfect or on which you can view changes being made as calculations are performed when using Lotus 1-2-3 or Joe Spreadsheet. The monitor is the visual display of your interaction with the computer. It is therefore an *output device*. Instructions from the application program appear on the screen so that you can make decisions about what step to perform next. You can also check the results of revisions you have made to a document. You input from the keyboard, and then see the results of the input on the screen.

The display or output on monitor screens is usually either *monochrome* (one color for the characters with another color for the background) or *color* (eight or more colors).

The Printer

The printer is an output device. Your computer communicates with your printer through a cable connection, much like your keyboard communicates with the computer. The kinds of printers linked to microcomputers vary greatly. Your instructor can tell you more about your printer and how to be certain that you are communicating correctly with it.

The output produced by your printer is often called *hard copy*. It is called hard copy because it is in a permanent form; it is tangible. An example of the opposite of hard copy, *soft copy,* would be the image of the document on your screen. Soft copy is temporary, but it is also considered output.

Secondary Storage

Earlier in this section you learned about the internal memory in your computer called RAM. RAM storage is temporary. When the power is turned off, everything contained in RAM is erased. For this reason, most data are stored semi-permanently on a *secondary storage medium*. A secondary storage medium is commonly some kind of *magnetic disk* such as one of the diskettes shown in Figure 1-1 or a rigid *hard disk*. Secondary storage devices such as a hard disk drive or a diskette drive, are the hardware components that write data to, or read data from, either the hard disk or the diskette. These devices are slower than RAM since they contain mechanical parts. Hard disks and diskettes will be discussed in depth later in this section.

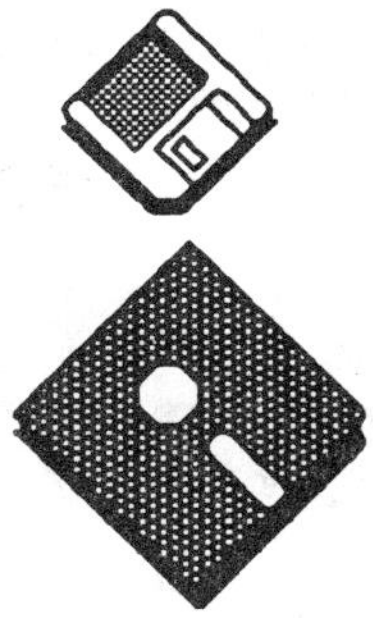

Figure 1-1. Diskettes

EXERCISE 1.2. HOW TO IDENTIFY PARTS OF THE KEYBOARD

The keyboard is an input device. It is used to put data into the computer. There are a variety of styles and sizes of keyboards available with computer systems. All keyboards, however, have several major features in common. They all have the standard alphabetic and numeric character keys in the center of the keyboard. One common arrangement is called the *QWERTY* keyboard because letters in the third row spell out QWERTY. The keyboard has the same arrangement as most typewriters. The keyboard is connected to the computer by a cable so that messages are sent directly to the computer's memory when keys are pressed. When you are typing a document or entering other data, the *cursor* appears on the screen at exactly the point where your next character will be inserted. The cursor is usually a flashing square or dash on the screen and moves as you enter characters or numeric figures.

Most keyboards also contain a numeric keypad. The numeric keypad may be used as a calculator and frequently doubles as the *cursor movement keys*, often called the *arrow keys*. The switch between numeric mode and the cursor movement keys is usually done with a key called the *Num Lock key*, located near the numeric keypad (See Figure 1-2).

Most keyboards also contain a set of *function keys*. These are labeled F1 through F10 (and occasionally higher) and are located either on the left side of the keyboard or across the top of the keyboard as shown in Figure 1-2 (a) and (b). Figure 1-1(a) shows the standard IBM PC keyboard with the function keys on the left and the numeric keypad on the right. You can see that the numeric keypad also contains arrows for the cursor movement as does (b) in Figure 1-2. Figure 1-2(b) shows the IBM PS/2 keyboard with function keys ranging from F1 through F12. It also contains an extra set of arrow keys in the middle of the keypad and some keys that perform similar functions to those in the numeric keypad. Frequently, the function keys are gray while other keys on the keyboard are white. This makes those keys that are used for specific tasks easy to locate. Several such keys are found on both the IBM PC and IBM PS/2 keyboards.

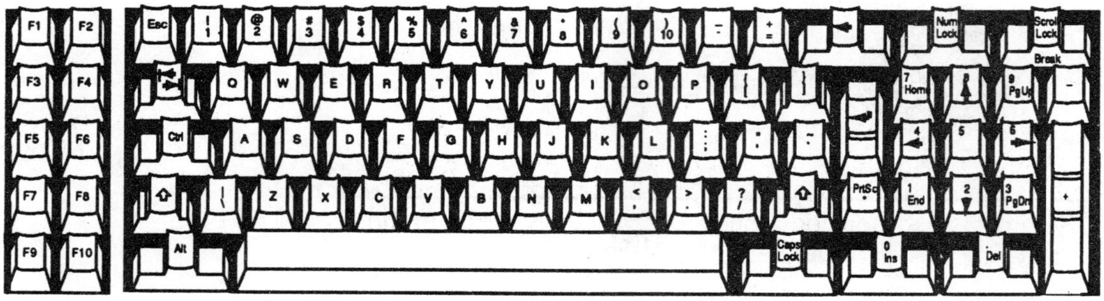

IBM PC Keyboard
(a)

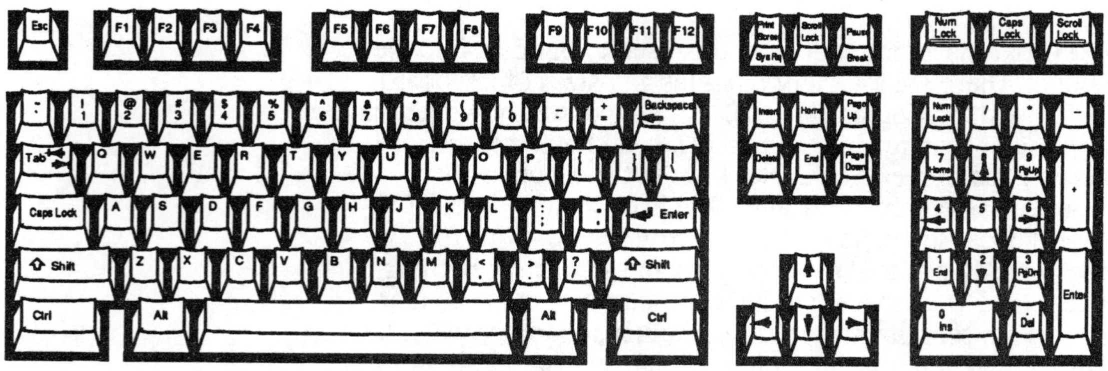

IBM PS/2 Keyboard
(b)

Figure 1-2. The IBM PC Keyboard (a) and the PS/2 Keyboard (b)

A few of the keys in Figure 1-2 are described next. Identify those on the diagram as they are discussed, and also look at the diagram to identify other keys and their locations on your keyboard.

The *Enter* or *Return* Key

Enter

↵

The *Enter* or *Return* key is used to initiate or invoke commands. It is pressed in response to a message on the screen or after keys are typed and is often thought of as the response or the conclusion of an action.

The *Arrow* Keys

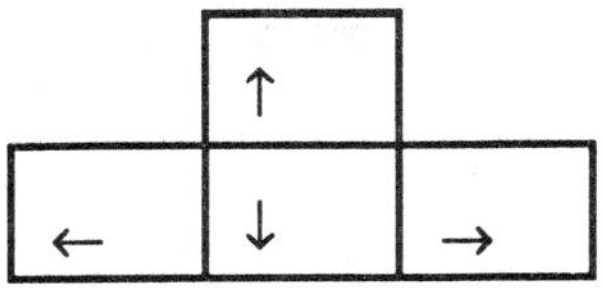

The *arrow* keys are used to move some pointer such as a blinking or solid cursor around the screen. They also move through text in all directions—forward, backward, left, and right. Regardless of their location, the arrow keys perform the same function.

The *Escape* Key

The *Escape* key is used in some programs to cancel a current action. While it is not used for this function in WordPerfect, it does allow you to cancel or backtrack out of messages and menus in Lotus 1-2-3, Joe Spreadsheet, and dBASE.

The *Delete* Key

The *Delete* key is used to remove the character at the cursor position. The character to the right then moves to the cursor position.

The *Insert* Key

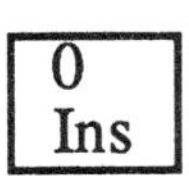

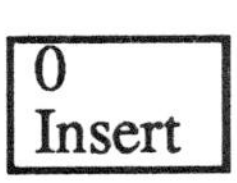

The *Insert* key allows you to insert characters at the cursor position and instructs that all characters to the right of the cursor be moved right (rather than typed over). It acts as a toggle between the Insert mode and the Typeover mode. By pressing it once, you can enter Typeover mode and be allowed to type on top of characters, thus replacing them. By pressing Insert again, you return to Insert mode and all text to the right of the cursor is moved right without the deletion of characters.

The *Backspace* Key

←

This key deletes characters to the left of the cursor position.

The *Shift, Ctrl, and Alt* Keys

Shift

⇑

Ctrl

Alt

These keys are used in combination with other keys to issue commands for the computer to do particular tasks. The *Shift*, *Ctrl*, or *Alt* key is always held down while the other key in the command is pressed. For example, in WordPerfect, holding the Shift key down, then quickly pressing the F6 key and releasing both will center text on a line between the two margins.

The *Num Lock* Key

Num
Lock

The *Num Lock* key is used to switch the numeric keypad between two uses as cursor movement keys or as a calculator. It is fairly easy to accidentally press the Num Lock key and get a string of numbers on the screen when you are trying to use the arrow keys to move the cursor. If this happens, simply press the Num Lock key again to return the use of the arrow keys.

The *Caps Lock* Key

Caps Lock

The *Caps Lock* key is used to produce uppercase letters on the keyboard without continually pressing the Shift key. By pressing the Caps Lock key once, all characters you type will show in uppercase. By pressing it again, all characters you type will be in lowercase, and the Shift key will be needed to type uppercase letters.

In addition to the keyboard, there are other types of input devices. A *Mouse* is often used to make selections from menus and to position the cursor. It replaces some of the functions of keystrokes on the keyboard by allowing the user to *point* to selections or to assign formats to text. The mouse may have a ball on its underside. Rolling the mouse around on a flat surface causes a pointer on the screen to move. When the pointer is in the correct position, clicking the button on the top side of the mouse completes a command or positions the cursor for text input.

For all exercises and instructions in this guide, you will be giving commands directly from the keyboard. While some PC programs are now using a mouse, these applications are not yet widespread. Also, it is important when operating any IBM-compatible computer to know what the keystrokes do and how they perform functions.

REVIEW QUESTIONS ON EXERCISES 1.1 AND 1.2

The following are diagrams of both the standard IBM keyboard and the PS/2 keyboard. Match each of the items listed below the diagrams to the correct location on the keyboard. If your keyboard varies a little from those shown, mark as closely as possible the correct location of each item on your keyboard.

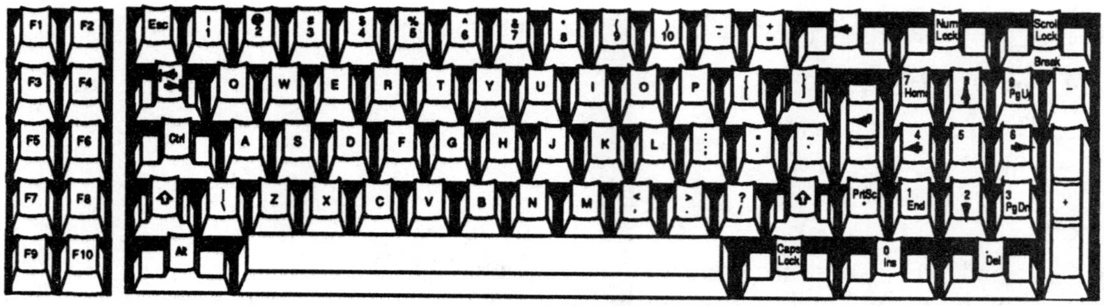

IBM PC Keyboard
(a)

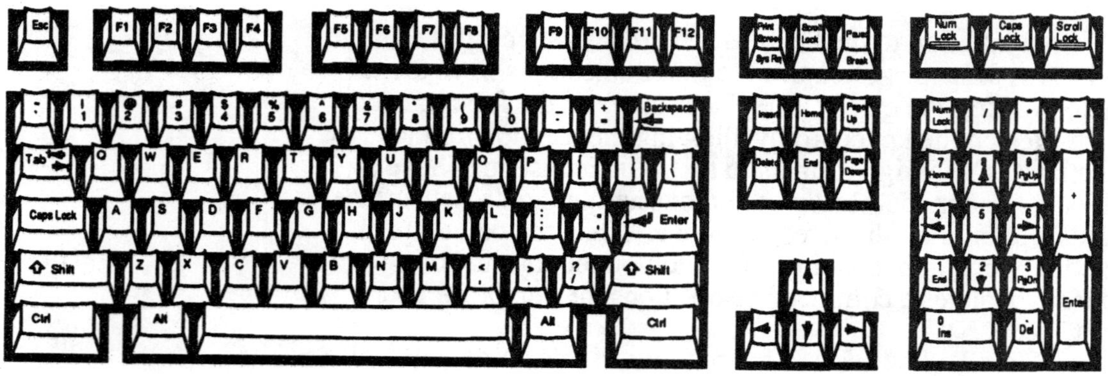

IBM PS/2 Keyboard
(b)

a. the function keys
b. the Esc key
c. the Return or Enter key
d. the Backspace key
e. the Shift keys
f. the Insert (Ins) key
g. the Del key
h. the Numeric keypad
i. the Num Lock key
j. the Alt key
k. the Ctrl key
l. the arrow keys
m. the Tab key
n. the Caps Lock key

Answer the following review questions. Fill in the answer in the blank and check your answers at the end of this exercise after completing all questions.

1. A computer system contains both ________ and ___________ parts.

2. Written programs stored on the hardware or on a diskette are called _____________.

3. Programs that do useful tasks for end-users of computers are called (two words) ____________ ___________.

4. The disk on which application software is contained is called the ______________________ disk.

5. The material you create with an application program is organized into ________.

Match each of the following hardware components to the correct definition stated below:

a. secondary storage
b. memory
c. keyboard
d. printer
e. microprocessor
f. monitor

6. ______ an output device used to create hard copy.

7. ______ where documents can be saved permanently without concern about power failure.

8. ______ an input device used to send messages to the computer.

9. ______ the internal storage section of a microcomputer.

10.______ the location of the CPU or Central Processing Unit.

11.______ the screen where output is displayed on a microcomputer.

Select the best answer for each of the following multiple-choice questions:

12. A diskette and a hard disk are examples of:

a. RAM
b. memory
c. secondary storage media
d. primary storage media

13. The Shift, Ctrl, or Alt keys:

a. work only by themselves and perform no other function
b. work by pressing them in conjunction with the spacebar
c. work by pressing them in conjunction with another key
d. work by pressing two of them together

14. The Del key removes text:

    a. to the left of the cursor
    b. only at the cursor position
    c. to the right of the cursor
    d. above or below the cursor position

15. The Num Lock key:

    a. changes the numeric keypad to a calculator-like keypad
    b. changes the numeric keypad to directional arrows on some keyboards
    c. acts as a toggle to switch between numeric mode and the arrow key mode
    d. all of the above
    e. none of the above

16. WordPerfect, Lotus 1-2-3 or Joe Spreadsheet, and dBASE III Plus are examples of:

    a. system software
    b. program languages
    c. application software
    d. programs stored permanently in ROM

Answers to Questions on Exercises 1.1 and 1.2

1. mechanical, electronic 2. software
3. application software 4. program 5. files
6. d 7. a 8. c 9. b 10. e 11. f 12. c
13. c 14. b 15. d 16. c

EXERCISE 1.3. HOW TO IDENTIFY MS- AND PC-DOS OPERATING SYSTEMS

An operating system is a set of programs that tells the computer system how to control resources, execute programs, and manage data. Application programs, such as WordPerfect, could not run on the computer without the operating system to guide them. When the DOS operating system is present, a symbol called a *prompt* appears on the screen. Depending on the type of computer in use (hard drive or dual-disk drives), the symbol will vary. It is, however, always a letter of the alphabet, such as:

A> (on a dual-disk system; See Figure 1-3)

or

C> (on a hard disk system)

(This prompt may vary somewhat.)

The system prompts are usually a letter of the alphabet, such as A, B, or C, followed by a "greater than" symbol (>). The A, B, or C indicates the *default* disk where the system software is located. When you see one of these prompts, you are at the operating system and are ready to give system commands or to load an application program into memory (RAM). The different kinds of prompts that may appear will be discussed later.

The operating systems common to IBM personal computers are MS-DOS (Microsoft Disk Operating System) or PC-DOS (Personal Computer Disk Operating System). In this guide, the operating system will be referred to simply as DOS.

DOS programs are stored on one or more diskettes and are usually purchased with the computer system. There are many programs stored on the DOS disk(s). They contain instructions for invoking certain commands which the user can access. You could read an entire book about all of the commands you can invoke using DOS; however, in this guide, you will learn only a few of the most commonly used commands—those you can start using immediately. First of all, you need to identify the kind of computer you are using and the location of DOS.

When using a hard disk system, DOS will probably be in a subdirectory of its own. A *directory* is a collection of files given a unique name, such as the DOS directory where all DOS files are located. More on this will be discussed later.

EXERCISE 1.4. HOW TO START THE COMPUTER

As you have read in this section, a computer system has several hardware components. One of the components you are now familiar with is RAM or random access memory. Some DOS programs are necessary for the operation of an application program such as WordPerfect or dBASE III Plus. These DOS programs must be stored in RAM prior to accessing an application program. Because the size of memory is limited, only the files needed for normal operation are loaded. These files are often referred to as *Internal* or *Resident* files. Other files that are not needed for the everyday operation of the computer remain on the DOS disk and are referred to as *External* or *Transient* files. Occasionally you may need to access the external files by invoking a command. When using DOS commands, you need to know whether they are in resident or transient files. Transient commands will require that your DOS disk be loaded in the appropriate drive.

Drive Configurations

There are two kinds of disk drives: diskette drives and hard disk drives. Look at Figure 1-3. It shows the possible drive configurations that come with IBM PCs and IBM-compatible (having a different vendor name but still able to use the same operating system and application software) systems.

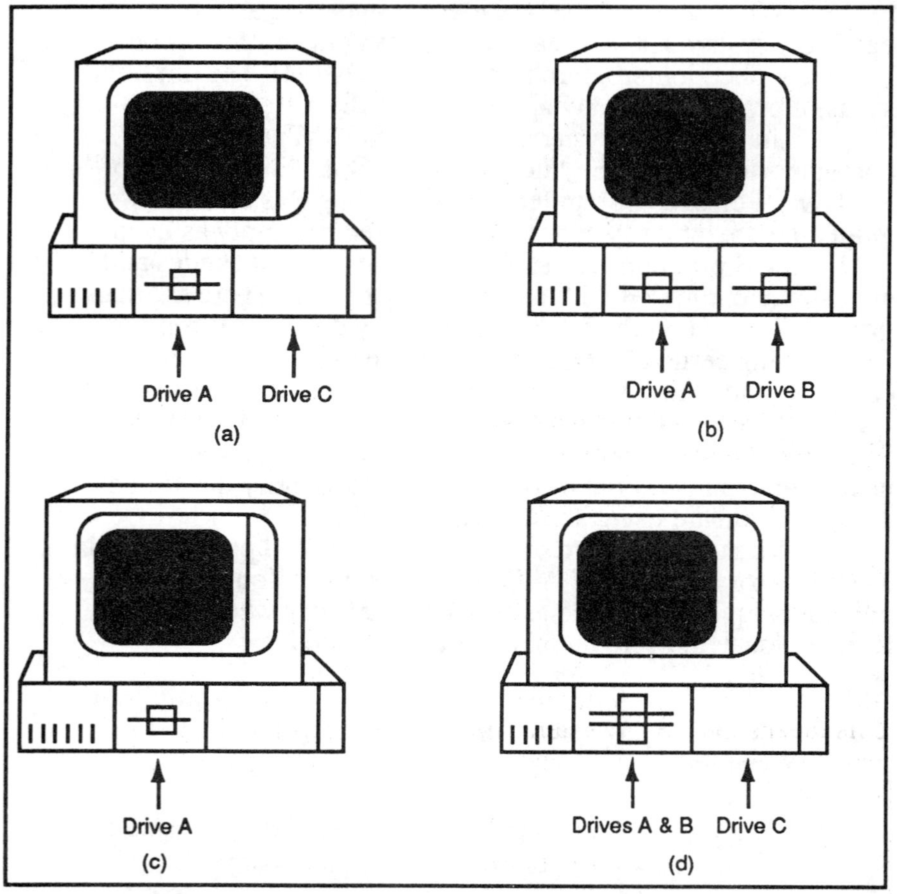

Figure 1-3. Disk-Drive Configurations

Diagram (a) shows a personal computer with a hard disk (Drive C) and a diskette drive (Drive A). Diagram (b) shows a dual-disk drive system (Drive A and Drive B). Diagram (c) shows a single diskette drive system (Drive A) with a diskette slot, and Diagram (d) shows a system with a hard drive (Drive C) and two diskette slots (Drives A and B). The most common configurations are either the dual-disk drive system or the hard disk system with one diskette slot. These two types of systems will be discussed in this guide. Generally speaking, when using a dual-disk system, first DOS and then the application program will be inserted into Drive A and your data disk (the disk containing the files you have created and want to save) will be located in Drive B. When using a hard disk and one diskette drive system, your program and DOS files may be stored permanently on the hard drive and your data (document) files will be saved on a diskette (the data disk) in Drive A.

There are two other possibilities concerning your diskette drives. Your computer may use either 5-1/4-inch or 3-1/2-inch diskettes.

If you have a *dual-disk system*, you will be using a version of DOS contained on a diskette. With the DOS diskette in hand:

1. Insert the DOS diskette into Drive A with the label facing up. If you are using 5-1/4-inch diskettes, the open slot showing the disk surface should be inserted first. If you are using the 3-1/2-inch diskettes, insert the disk in the direction of the arrow on the surface of the disk.

2. Close the drive door

3. Turn the computer on

If you are using a *hard disk system* with one diskette drive, all you need to do is:

1. Turn the computer on

Your system files are contained on Drive C and will automatically *boot* (load into memory) when the computer is turned on.

You will hear some whirring noises inside your computer and in a few moments will see a date and time prompt. This means that some system files have been loaded into memory. When you start your system with DOS, you in essence boot your computer.

Figure 1-4 shows a date and time message on a screen. At this time, you see only the first two lines on your screen. It is not necessary to enter the date and time each time you sign on, but doing so allows the correct date and time to appear when files are created or updated. This information can be helpful when you later view the files in a directory (discussed later in this section).

Especially if you are using a hard disk system, you may not need to enter the current date and time each time you sign on. Frequently the date and time are preset and will remain accurate. If you want to make a change in the date and time, however, follow the steps listed below the figure.

```
Current date is Fri 10-26-1990
Enter new date (mm-dd-yy):
Current time is 11:07:37.32
Enter new time:
```

Figure 1-4. Date and Time Messages

You must type the date and time in exactly the format shown on your screen. Notice that the second line shows a format in parentheses of: mm-dd-yy. This means that you must type the date as figures separated by hyphens. You can use a single figure or double figures. If the month or day is 1 through 9, for example, it is not necessary to enter a zero in front of the number. You could simply type: 1-8-90.

1. Type the current date

2. Press **Enter** or Return when finished

NOTE: From now on, the Enter or Return key will be referred to as Enter.

The time prompt now appears. You enter the time by typing the hour and minutes separated by a colon, such as: 11:07.

3. Type the current time

4. Press **Enter** when finished

NOTE: If you make an error, a new date or time prompt may appear so that you can type the entry again.

When you press Enter after typing the time, you will see either an A> (A prompt) when using a dual-disk system or a C> (C prompt) when using a hard disk system.

EXERCISE 1.5. HOW TO USE DOS COMMANDS

Once you are at the DOS prompt, you are ready to give DOS commands. As mentioned earlier, those covered in this guide are but a few of the many commands you can invoke using DOS. They are, however, some of the most frequently used commands, and you will want to be familiar with them for future use. You can view some of these commands by looking at a list of files contained on the DOS disk. The combination of these files is called the *DOS directory*. To view the directory,

From a dual-disk system:

1. Type **DIR** at the A>

2. Press **Enter**

From a hard disk system:

You will use a similar process to that used in a dual-disk system; however, the drive locations and the location of the DOS directory will change. You may need to check with your instructor to confirm the location and the name of the DOS directory. Use the following procedure if DOS files are not in a separate subdirectory.

1. Start at the hard disk system prompt, C>

2. Type **DIR**

If DOS files are in a separate subdirectory, substitute the DOS directory name on your system for "DOS" in the steps below.

1. Type **CD DOS**

2. Press **Enter**

You will see a DOS directory prompt similar to the following:

C:\DOS>

3. Type **DIR** and press **Enter**

You will see a directory similar to the partial one shown in Figure 1-5. (Hard disk users will see information on the C drive and the DOS directory at the top of the screen rather than the A drive information.)

Volume in A drive has no label
Directory of A:\

COMMAND	COM	23210	3-07-85	2:23p
ANSI	SYS	1651	3-07-85	2:23p
ASSIGN	COM	1509	3-07-85	2:23p
.				
.				
.				
	48 file(s)		14336 bytes free	

Figure 1-5. Partial DOS Directory

Look closely at your list of DOS files. The name of the file contains two parts—shown in the first and second columns on your screen. The first part is the filename; the second part is the file extension. Looking at the example in Figure 1-5, the first filename is COMMAND and its file extension is COM. The filename is written as COMMAND.COM. The filename and extension appear differently when listed in a directory than when you type them. In typing, the period is used to show separation between the filename and its extension. Filenames are anywhere from one to eight characters in length, and it is *IMPORTANT* to remember when creating filenames that they may contain numbers or characters but may *NOT* contain spaces. The file extensions are always one to three characters (or numbers) in length with three characters most often used.

The middle column shown in Figure 1-5 and on your directory contains the total number of bytes used in the file. The fourth and fifth columns show the date and time the file was created. You can see the advantage of knowing the date and time of the file creation. When you look at this directory, the directory of your data disk, or another disk directory, the format will look similar. At the bottom of your list of files is a message showing the total number of files on your DOS disk and the total number of bytes free on this disk (or the total bytes remaining on your hard disk).

You can use different variations of the DIR command to see a copy of a directory. At your system prompt, you could type:

DIR/W

to see a copy of the directory across the width of your screen. This command eliminates some of the file information however. Only the filename and extension are displayed so that more files can be displayed across the width. The information at the bottom of the screen (total files and bytes free) will remain the same.

As you may have noticed, when the directory gets too long, some of the files may disappear from the screen. To view only a screen or page of files at a time, you could type:

DIR/P

at the system prompt. A message will appear at the bottom of the screen telling you to "Strike a key" when you are ready to view the next page.

The FORMAT Command

The FORMAT command is one of the most used and most important of the DOS commands. It is used every time you buy a new blank diskette. The FORMAT command is used to prepare a new diskette for receiving files. It sets up a directory, marks off sectors (storage areas), and tests the tracks on the surface of the diskette to be sure that data can be stored on them. The tracks are similar to the grooves in a record, and the sectors are divisions similar to pieces in a pie. The sectors and tracks are designated storage areas on the surface of the disk.

You need to format the diskette only once. If you give the FORMAT command to a diskette containing data documents, it will erase the contents of the diskette. If you want to do this, then use FORMAT; otherwise, be very careful to use it only when preparing a new diskette.

From a dual-disk system:

1. Insert a new diskette in Drive B (usually on the right or bottom) with the label up and the open slot to the back of the drive (or in the direction of the arrow on the 3-1/2-inch diskette). Be sure the DOS diskette is in the A drive.

2. Close the drive doors

3. At the A>, type:

   FORMAT B:

NOTE: You may use either upper- or lowercase letters. In this guide you will see uppercase letters used for clarity.

4. Press **Enter**

A message appears asking you to place a blank diskette in B. The message will then ask you to press any key or the Enter key (depending upon your DOS version) when you are sure the diskette is correctly inserted.

5. Press **Enter** or any key (whichever you are asked to do by the screen message)

You will hear a whirring sound and will see the light turn on the

B drive. Wait until the formatting process is complete and until you are prompted with the message:

Format another (Y/N)?

6. Press **N** for No

7. Press **Enter**

Your screen shows the system prompt again.

With a hard disk system:

1. At the DOS prompt (C>), type:

   FORMAT A:

2. Press **Enter**

3. You will see a message on the screen asking you to be sure to insert the blank diskette in Drive A. Do this now. Insert the diskette with the label up and the open slot to the back (or in the direction of the arrow on the surface of the diskette if using a 3-1/2-inch diskette). Close the drive door.

4. Press **Enter** or any key (whichever the screen message is asking for) when the diskettes are ready

You will hear a whirring sound and see the light come on the A drive. Wait until you see another message on the screen that says:

Format another (Y/N)?

5. Press **N** for No

6. Press **Enter** to return to the DOS prompt (DOS>)

7. Now return to the system prompt by typing

   CD

8. Press **Enter**

You will return to the C>.

To Users of Both Dual and Hard Disk Systems: At this point you could turn your computer off and boot again at the next session. You are ready to turn your computer off when you have returned to the A> on a dual-disk system or the C> on a hard disk system. These prompts will always be your starting and ending messages. You should always see a system prompt when the system is correctly booted, and you should always see one when you have finished using the computer before turning the system off.

The Logged Drive

The prompt showing on the screen, such as A> or C> displays your *logged drive*. When you use commands such as the DIR command to see the contents of the drive, you are looking at the contents of the logged drive. You can view the contents of other drives (for example, the B drive on a dual-disk system or the A drive on a hard disk system) by giving another command.

NOTE: From this point on in the guide, it will be assumed that you know that if you are using a hard disk system your formatted disk (later to contain your data documents) will be in the A drive, and that if you are using a dual-disk system, your formatted disk will be in Drive B. It will also be assumed that you know that you are operating from Drive C with a hard disk system and from Drive A with a dual-disk system.

1. From your current logged drive, either A or C, and with a formatted disk in either the B drive or A drive, respectively, type:

   DIR B: (if using dual-disk drives)

   or

   DIR A: (if using a hard disk)

2. Press **Enter**

You will see information concerning the amount of bytes remaining on the disk, and a line at the bottom of your screen will show the date and time of formatting. At this time there are no data documents so you will see the message, "Bad command or filename."

When you give the above command, you remain logged onto Drive A or C. This means that after the directory information is displayed, you are returned to the original system prompt (A or C). You also have the option of changing the logged drive and thus changing the prompt.

1. At the A or C prompt, type:

   B: (dual-disk)

   or

   A: (hard disk)

2. Press **Enter**

A B> or A> appears. You have now changed the logged drive. At this point you can look at the directory of the drive by typing DIR and pressing Enter; however, there is little else you can do. You cannot, for instance, give any *external* DOS commands such as the FORMAT command. Your DOS disk is contained back in Drive A or in another directory on Drive C, and you must be logged onto that drive in order to access those commands. If you tried giving the FORMAT command at the B or A prompt, you wouldn't get very far. A message would appear telling you that the files could not be found.

3. Change the logged drive back to A or C by typing:

   A: (dual-disk)

   or

   C: (hard disk)

The COPY Command

One of the most useful DOS commands is the *COPY* command. You use the COPY command to copy files from one disk to another. You have the option of copying one, some, or all of your disk files. There are many reasons you may want to make copies from one disk to another. You may want to transfer a file to another disk containing related files, or you may simply want to make a backup copy of a file. If you are making backup copies to another disk, and that disk is new, you will need to be sure that it is formatted. If you are copying to a disk that already contains some files, all you need to do is give the COPY command.

Before you use the COPY command, you need to be at the system prompt (either A for a dual-diskette system or C for the hard disk system). The COPY command is an *internal* DOS command, so you do not need to have the DOS disk in Drive A or be at the DOS prompt when using a hard disk system.

For this exercise, you will copy one of the DOS files to your formatted disk. This is for educational practice purposes only, and you will be instructed to erase the file at the end of this exercise. In general, the COPY command should not be used on copyrighted software such as DOS.

1. Insert the DOS disk in Drive A or be sure you are at the C> if using a hard disk system

2. Insert your formatted data disk in Drive B (dual-disk) or in Drive A (hard disk)

3. At the A> or C>, type:

COPY COMMAND.COM B: (use **A**: instead when using a hard disk)

NOTE: COMMAND.COM is one of the files on your DOS disk. You can view this file by giving the DIR.

This command copies the file COMMAND.COM from the logged drive (A or C in this case) to the disk in Drive B or A. Note also that the filename includes the extension. When you are copying from one disk to another, be sure to include the entire name with the period separating the filename and the file's extension.

If you make an error in the spacing or typing of the filenames, simply backspace to correct the error and retype it.

4. Press **Enter** when the line is correctly typed

A message will appear when the copying process is complete. It will say, "1 File(s) copied."

At times you may want to copy more than one document. Suppose for example that you wanted to copy all files with the extension of .COM to another disk. (A more likely possibility might be that you would want to copy all WordPerfect files with an extension of .WP1, which you might enter when you save some of your WordPerfect documents. For this exercise, though, you will practice by copying the .COM files from the DOS disk.)

1. At the A> or C>, type:

   COPY *.COM B: (or **A**: with a hard disk)

2. Press **Enter**

This command copies all files from the default drive (A or C, respectively) to the data disk in B or A with filename extensions of COM. The asterisk (*) is recognized as a *wildcard* or *global character* and will thus pick all files with the extension COM regardless of the filename.

If you wrote a command like the one above but, changed the position of the asterisk (*), you could copy all similar filenames with different extensions, such as:

COPY LETTER.* B: (or A:)

One other variation of this command is:

COPY *.* B:

As with the other commands, the asterisk (*) is a global character, and in this command will copy all files regardless of the filename or the extension.

As you practice more with creating and saving

documents, you will become more comfortable with organizing your documents by extension names. For example, you may want all memos to have an extension of MEM or all letters to have an extension of LET. The possibilities of one-to three-character extensions are limited only to the combinations of letters and figures you can arrange in three characters.

The DISKCOPY Command

The DISKCOPY command is similar to the COPY *.* command in that it copies all files from one disk to another. There are, however, some major differences between the two commands. The DISKCOPY command erases the contents of the target disk (the disk in Drive B or A). It also formats a new disk before copying files. These could be either good or bad features, depending upon how you look at them. Use the DISKCOPY command when you have a new disk, unformatted, onto which you want to copy the entire contents of another disk. But be careful NOT to use this command to copy files onto a disk with contents you want to save. For that function, use the COPY command.

The DISKCOPY command also copies all of the features of the disk, including bad sectors or tracks. If you think the disk may be bad, copy necessary files to another disk using the COPY command.

For this exercise, you will copy the entire contents of the DOS disk onto your disk in Drive B or A. There are not any important files on your data disk that you want to save, so this exercise will not erase any valuable data. Please note that copying the contents of the DOS disk is for practice purposes only, and you will be instructed to erase the copy at the end of this exercise. You should not use the COPY command on copyrighted software.

The DISKCOPY command is an *external* command so you need to work from DOS before using the command.

1. Insert the DOS disk into Drive A (dual-disk system)

   or

   Change to the DOS prompt (C:\DOS>) (hard disk)

NOTE: Hard disk users, type: **CD DOS** at the C> to change to the DOS directory.

2. With the data disk in Drive B or A, type:

   DISKCOPY A: B: (dual-disk)

3. Press **Enter** when the line is typed correctly

You will see a message on the screen that asks you to be sure the source and target disks are in the correct location and then to press Enter or any key (depending on the DOS version) when ready.

4. Press **Enter** or any key (whichever you are asked to do by the screen message)

Wait while the contents of the disk are copied. When the process is finished, a message will appear asking whether you want to copy another.

5. Type **N** for No (to the message asking whether you want to copy another)

If you wish, you can now view the contents of the disk in Drive B or A by typing either DIR B: or DIR A: at the system prompt. You will see that the DOS disk has been copied.

The ERASE Command

The ERASE command will erase one, some, or all files from a disk. The ERASE command needs to be used with caution. Be certain that you want to erase files *permanently* before using this command.

This command is useful for erasing unwanted files from your disk. Sometimes files are accidentally saved under different but similar filenames when the contents of the files are exactly the same. Occasionally a data file is accidentally saved on the DOS disk. In these instances, you can erase the unwanted files from the disk and thus "clean" the disk so that you have more room to save files you create in the future.

The ERASE command is an *internal* command so you do not need to be at a DOS prompt or have the DOS disk inserted in Drive A to give this command. It will have the same effect also if you give it from an A> or a B> or a C> system prompt.

With your data disk (now containing DOS files) in Drive B or Drive A, do the following:

1. First, look at the directory, by typing,

   DIR B: (dual disk)

   or

   DIR A: (hard disk)

2. Press **Enter**

You can see that one of your files is the COMMAND.COM file. Practice erasing this file by typing the following command:

3. Type

   ERASE B:COMMAND.COM (dual disk)

   or

   ERASE A:COMMAND.COM (hard disk)

Be careful to type in the correct drive designation (either A or B). If you typed "ERASE A:" with a dual-disk system, you could erase parts of the DOS disk.

4. Press **Enter**

A message will tell you that one file has been erased. Once again, the asterisk (*) command can act as a global command so that you can erase selected files. You could substitute the filename or the file extension with the * and thus erase groups of files. Similarly, the *.* command will erase all files.

Type the following command:

5. **ERASE B:*.*** (dual disk)

   or

   ERASE A:*.* (hard disk)

6. Press **Enter**

Screen will ask, "Are you sure (Y/N)?"

7. Press **Y** for yes

NOTE: It cannot be emphasized enough to use caution when employing the ERASE command. Use it primarily for erasing individual files that are no longer of use to you. If you want to erase the contents of the disk, be sure to check every filename before doing so. Once the ERASE command is executed, the files will be erased. If you erase files by mistake, check with your instructor to see if they can be restored.

REVIEW QUESTIONS ON EXERCISES 1.3, 1.4, AND 1.5

Fill in the BEST answer to each of the following questions.

1. The operating systems common to the IBM personal computer are ______________ and ____________.

2. There are many ____________ stored on the DOS disk(s).

3. DOS programs necessary for the everyday operation of the computer are stored in _______ whenever the computer is being used.

4. Some DOS files that are not necessary for normal computer operation are referred to as ____________ because they remain on the DOS disk until needed.

5. Types of DOS files are both ___________ and ____________.

6. The DOS disk must be in the drive before using ___________ DOS commands.

7. Your disk drive configuration is _____________.

8. Your DOS files are usually located in Drive _______________.

9. Your data disk is usually located in Drive ______________.

10. Your diskette size is ____________.

Choose the BEST answer for the following multiple-choice questions:

(This question is for dual-disk users only.)

11. Which of the following is the correct procedure used to "boot" your system?

    a. Insert the DOS disk into Drive A with the label facing down and the slot to the back; close the drive door; turn on the computer.
    b. Insert DOS into Drive A with the label facing up and the slot to the back; close the drive door; turn on the computer.
    c. Turn on the computer; insert DOS into Drive A; close the drive door.
    d. None of the above.

12. The Date and Time prompts appear

    a. after the A> (or C>)
    b. after looking at the directory of files
    c. after booting with DOS
    d. after booting with DOS and pressing Enter

13. To view a directory of files on a disk, you would type

    a. DIR and press Enter
    b. DIR/W and press Enter
    c. DIR B: and press Enter (or DIR A: with a hard disk)
    d. any of the above
    e. none of the above

14. A directory shows which of the following:

    a. the filename, extension, size of the file, and date and time of its creation
    b. the filename, extension, and size only
    c. the filename, extension, and date only
    d. the filename, size, date, and type of system used

15. The command DIR/P does which of the following?

    a. prints a copy of the directory
    b. prints a page of the directory
    c. shows a page of the directory
    d. prints the size of the directory

Answer each of the following True/False questions with a T or an F. Decide the BEST answer for each.

16. _____ The FORMAT command is primarily used to prepare a new disk for receiving data files.

17. _____ Accidentally formatting a disk would not erase the disk contents.

18. _____ If you see an A> or a B> or a C> on your screen, this prompt displays the "logged" drive.

19. _____ The COPY command copies only single files at a time from one disk to another.

20. _____ The DISKCOPY command is frequently used to copy the entire contents of one disk to another without losing the contents of the target disk.

Answers to Questions on Exercises 1.3, 1.4, and 1.5

1. MS-DOS and PC-DOS 2. files 3. RAM 4. external 5. internal and external 6. external 7. either single diskette, dual-diskette, hard disk with two diskette drives, or hard disk with one diskette drive 8. on a diskette or on the hard disk in a directory of its own 9. in either the B drive or the A drive depending on the system configuration 10. either 5-1/4 or 3-1/2 11. b 12. c 13. d 14. a 15. c 16. T 17. F 18. T 19. F 20. F

COMMAND SUMMARY

To start the computer

With a hard disk system:

1. Turn the system on *without* a disk in Drive A. DOS is contained on the hard disk.

2. At the date and time prompts, type the correct date and time (if necessary), and press **Enter** after each entry

You will see the system prompt (C>).

With a dual-disk system:

1. Insert the DOS disk in Drive A

2. Turn the system on. Type the correct date and time entries, and press **Enter** when finished.

You will then see the A> on your screen.

To view the file or disk directory

1. At the system prompt (A>, C>, or B>), type:

   DIR and press **Enter**

Other DIR commands (entered at the system prompt):

a. Type **DIR/W** to see a list of filenames across the width of the screen

b. Type **DIR/P** to see filenames listed on a screen a page at a time

c. Type **DIR B:** to see the B drive's directory

The FORMAT command

Use this command to format a new diskette or to erase the entire contents of the disk.

<u>With a hard disk system:</u>

Be sure the disk to be formatted is in Drive A with the drive door closed.

1. Change to the DOS directory by typing:

   CD DOS (assuming your DOS directory is called DOS)

2. Press **Enter**

3. At the DOS prompt (C:/DOS>), type:

   FORMAT A:

4. Press **Enter**

A message will appear asking you to be sure that you have a disk in the correct drive (A).

5. Press **Enter** or any key (depending upon your DOS version—follow the screen message)

6. WAIT for the FORMAT process to finish

When it is finished, you will see the message:

Format another (Y/N)?

7. Respond by pressing **Y** for Yes, or **N** for No

8. Press **Enter** to continue

When you are through formatting, go back to the system prompt by typing:

CD

at the DOS>.

With a dual-disk system:

1. Leave (or insert) your DOS disk in Drive A

2. Insert the new disk in Drive B

3. At the A>, type:

   FORMAT B:

4. Press **Enter**

A message will appear asking you to insert the target disk in Drive B. You have done this, so continue.

5. Press **Enter**

6. WAIT for the FORMAT process to be completed. When it is, you will see the message:

   Format another (Y/N)?

7. Respond with **Y** for Yes or **N** for No

8. Press **Enter**

When you are through using the FORMAT command and have selected N, you will return to the system prompt (A>).

The logged drive

Use this command to change from one logged drive (such as A or C) to another drive (such as B or A).

With a hard disk:

1. At the C>, type:

   A:

2. Press **Enter**

The prompt will change to A>.

With a dual-disk system:

1. At the A>, type:

   B:

2. Press **Enter**

NOTE: If you have simply changed drives by typing B: or A: and pressing Enter, and you want to change logged drives back to A or C, simply type the logged drive followed by a colon and press Enter. Do this at the B or A prompt.

The COPY command

Use the command to copy file(s) from one disk (or directory) to another. Give the COPY command at the system prompt from which you want to copy. If using a dual-diskette system, insert the target disk into Drive B. Be sure to use the filename and extension.

To copy a single file:

1. Type:

   COPY filename.ext B: (or **A:** with a hard disk)

To copy files with the same extensions and any filename:

1. Type:

   COPY *.EXT B: (or A: with a hard disk)

2. Press **Enter**

To copy files with the same filename and any extension:

1. Type:

   COPY NAME.* B: (or **A:**)

2. Press **Enter**

To copy all files:

1. Type:

   COPY *.* B: (or **A:**)

2. Press **Enter**

The DISKCOPY command

Use this command to copy all contents from one disk to another and to erase the contents of the target disk at the same time. For this command, your DOS disk must be in Drive A if using a dual disk system or you must be at the DOS prompt when using a hard disk system.

1. From the prompt containing the sources files, type:

   DISKCOPY A: B:

2. Press **Enter**

Respond to the message when the DISKCOPY process is over.

The ERASE command

Be VERY CAREFUL with this command. It can erase the entire contents of your disk. Use it to erase one, some, or all files. Be sure you are at the prompt for the directory containing the files to be erased.

<u>To ERASE a single file</u>:

1. Type:

   ERASE filename.ext

2. Press **Enter**

<u>To ERASE all files</u>:

1. Type:

   ERASE *.*

2. Press **Enter**

NOTE: You can also erase the contents of Drive B or Drive A (hard disk) while giving the command from Drive A or Drive C, respectively. To do so, just add the drive followed by a colon after the ERASE command, such as: ERASE B:*.*

NOTES

SECTION 2

WORD PROCESSING

PREVIEW

A word processing software program is one that allows you to type documents such as letters and memos, make quick and easy corrections when necessary, store the text so that it is permanently saved, and access the text again whenever you want to make revisions. It also allows you to print the text in a number of formats. With a word processing program, you can delete, insert, move, copy, and merge text (to name only a few of the functions) without the necessity of retyping.

In this section you will learn to use WordPerfect. WordPerfect is one of the most well-known and most widely used word processing packages. It is an extremely powerful program that is also reasonably easy to learn and operate. You will be learning many of these functions in this section. Some of them are:

How to type a short document

How to store and print a document

How to make editing revisions

How to format a document to improve its appearance

How to adjust line and page formatting

How to make automatic headings on every page of a long document

USING THIS GUIDE

The instructions presented in this section are for both WordPerfect 4.2 and 5.0. Where the menus and/or options change in 5.0, mention is made of how the menu will appear and what changes occur.

As you are working through this section (and Sections 3 and 4), you will see a number of exercises. The functions presented are divided into several short exercises, such as Exercise 2.1, "How to Start and Quit." Each of the exercises contains step-by-step instructions on exactly what to do to when practicing the feature at your computer. Work through each of these steps. At the end of most of the exercises is a list of review questions. These questions are included to help you quickly recall the steps just presented in the exercise and to help you formulate the answers in your own words. The best way to retain the knowledge is to think the process through immediately after it is presented and put those thoughts down on paper. In this way you will also have a handy reference sheet to use as you become more competent in using WordPerfect. Answers are given at the end of each set of review questions. It is, of course, is highly recommended that you work through all of the questions first, and when completely satisfied with your answers, check the answers supplied at the end.

At the end of each exercise, you have the option of either continuing to the next exercise or stopping. Your schedule will determine where you will finish.

A "Command Summary" is included at the end of this section (as it is in each section in this guide). It is a summary of the steps used to complete the most frequently used functions presented in the section. Because it is brief (with only the keystrokes listed), it is recommended that you not refer to this section as a learning guide, but only as a reference after having completed the more detailed instructions in the exercises.

BEGINNING WORDPERFECT FUNCTIONS

EXERCISE 2.1. HOW TO START AND QUIT

In this exercise you will learn how to load WordPerfect into your working memory (RAM—see Section 1) and how to leave the program when you are ready to quit using WordPerfect. These two steps are the most important in starting and ending a session with WordPerfect.

The first thing you will need to do is be certain you have all of the necessary tools. They are:

a. a diskette containing the WordPerfect program
(if using a dual-disk system)

b. a formatted data disk on which to store your documents
(both dual- and hard disk users)
(See Section 1 for formatting)

NOTE to hard disk users: If you are using a hard disk system, you may not need the program disk. The WordPerfect program will most likely be stored on your C Drive in its own directory. You may need to check with the instructor to find out the exact name of the directory. For reference in this guide, it will be assumed that it is called WP for WordPerfect. Instructions for changing to that directory and loading the program follow.

To Load the Program

For both dual-disk and hard disk users, you will need to boot the system and be at the system prompt (either A> or C:\>).

<u>From a dual-disk system</u>:

1. Insert the WordPerfect program disk into Drive A
2. Insert your data disk into Drive B
3. Close the drive doors
4. Type **WP** at the A>
5. Press **Enter**
6. Press any key after reading the copyright and informational screen

<u>From a hard disk system</u>:

With your data disk in Drive A,

1. Change to the WordPerfect directory (check with your instructor as to the exact directory name), by typing:

   CD WP (for Change Directory Word Perfect)

   at the system prompt (C:\>)
2. Press **Enter**
3. At the WordPerfect directory prompt, C:\WP>, type:

   WP
4. Press **Enter**
6. Press any key after reading the copyright and informational screen

<u>For both dual- and hard disk users</u>:

The screen you will see in 4.2 is shown in Figure 2-1.

Figure 2-1. Opening WordPerfect Screen

The Status Line

Your screen is blank except for a *cursor* in the upper left corner and a line of information in the lower right corner. This line is called the *status line*. The status line is used primarily to provide information about the cursor's current location. It also provides other information, at times, about the type of format in use, warnings, and other prompts (discussed later in this section).

Looking more closely at the status line, the information you see there tells you the following:

Doc 1: This notation tells you which document you are working on. WordPerfect can retain two files in its memory at the same time. If you think of this file as a sheet of paper on a desktop, this is then Document 1. You might also want to have another document on your desktop and have the ability to look at one or the other quickly. The second document would show the notation Doc 2.

It might happen that you accidentally load two documents into your working memory. If this happens and you are not sure where your original document is, just check the status line. You can switch back to Doc 1 quickly by simply pressing the F3 key once. This key acts as a toggle between the two open documents.

Pg 1: The *Pg* notation shows you on which page in your document your cursor is located. If you were typing a long document and were currently on Page 3 of the document, the notation would read Pg 3.

Ln 1: The *Ln* notation tells you the position (in inches in 5.0) of the line where the cursor is currently located. This notation will change as you either type text or press the Enter key.

Pos 1: The *Pos* notation shows the current position of your cursor. You will see either a 10 as the position or a 1 (4.2 and 5.0, respectively). WordPerfect automatically leaves a 1-inch left margin, so when you are at the far left edge of your document, you are at the 1-inch position. This will appear as a Position 10 figure or as a 1-inch figure depending upon the version you are using. Each time you press the spacebar or type a character, the Pos notation will change.

1. Type **your name and address** now in three short lines as shown below. Start with the cursor in the upper left corner of the screen and press the **Enter** key after each line. Press **Enter** several times after the last line (Do not worry about errors).

   name
   address
   city state zip

   As you are typing, watch the status line change. You should see changes in the Line and Pos location.

2. Press the **arrow keys** to move around through text and watch as the status line changes as your cursor position changes.

The Function Keys

For just a moment, look away from your screen to your function keys. You should have a 4.2 or 5.0 template. It is not important at this time that you go through each of the functions available through the use of the function keys in WordPerfect. What is important is that you realize the important role the function keys play in performing tasks with WordPerfect. Most software programs have built-in tasks that are performed through the function keys, but what these tasks are and which keys they use varies from program to program. In WordPerfect, the important thing to remember is that you use the function keys either alone or in combination with another key. The other keys are: the *Ctrl* key, the *Shift* key, and the *Alt* key. When you use one of these three keys with a function key, you hold down the key, then press the function key, and finally release both keys. The command to print, for example, is Shift F7. This means that you must hold down the Shift key first, then press the F7 key, and then release both keys. You will notice on the template that the words "Ctrl," "Shift," and "Alt" are located in the upper left corner of the template and that they are printed in different colors. "Ctrl" is printed in red, "Shift" is printed in green, and "Alt" is printed in blue. Look at your template and notice that words located on the left or right of a function key are also color coded. Of course, you use the appropriate key to match the color for the function. Look again at the F7 key. Note that the Print command is in green; thus you would use the Shift F7 command to get to this particular print menu.

As you progress through this section, many of the functions on the template will be presented using several combinations of the keys. If the word appears in black next to the function key, you may reach that menu by pressing the function key alone.

To EXIT the Program

One of the most frequently used function keys is the F7 key. It is used to both clear the screen and exit the program. For now, you are going to practice simply exiting the program.

1. Look at the F7 function key template list

The word "Exit" appears in black at the bottom of the list of tasks.

2. Press **F7**

A message appears on the screen asking whether you want to save your document. This one was just for practice, so

3. Type **N** for No

4. Now type **Y** for Yes

to the message asking whether you want to exit.

NOTE: If you had replied N to the prompt asking whether you wanted to exit, you would have returned to a blank WordPerfect document space. This is the procedure used to clear the screen, without exiting the program.

You are now back at a system prompt, and you may continue to the review questions and the next exercise, or quit.

REVIEW QUESTIONS ON EXERCISE 2.1

1. List some of the things you can do with a word processing program.

2. List the steps necessary to load WordPerfect into memory.

3. What does each of the following status line remarks tell you?

Doc 1

Pg 1

Ln 1

Pos 1

4. There are four tasks listed opposite each one of your function keys. Why are they color coded? What key is used with each color?

5. What are the two functions of the word "Exit" on the F7 key?

Answers to the Review Questions on Exercise 2.1

1. Type documents, edit them quickly, save them permanently, revise them, print a copy. All without the need of retyping the document.

2. dual-disk:

   a. WP Program disk in A
   b. Data disk in B
   c. Type **WP** at the A>

hard disk:

a. Change to the WordPerfect directory
b. Data disk in A
c. Type **WP** at the WP directory prompt

3. Doc 1 — On which document you are working (your cursor is located in) of 2 possible active documents

   Pg 1 — In which page your cursor is located

   Ln 1 — On which line your cursor is located (measured in inches for WordPerfect 5.0 or in lines for 4.2)

   Pos 1 — In which position your cursor is located (as it moves across the screen)

4. They are color coded so that a secondary key may be used in conjunction with the function key. Black means to use the function key alone; red means to use Ctrl; green means to use Shift; and blue means to use Alt.

5. To exit WordPerfect or to clear the screen.

EXERCISE 2.2. HOW TO CREATE A SHORT DOCUMENT

1. Load WordPerfect

In this exercise you will create a short letter (shown on the following page). As you are typing, you should note the following:

Word wrap: As you reach the right margin when typing the paragraphs, DO NOT press the Enter key. With WordPerfect and many other word processing programs, the text you are entering will reach the right margin, and, as you continue typing, will wrap automatically to the next line. The only times you need to press the Enter key are when you want to force the text to the next line, such as in the address and on the date line, or at the end of a paragraph.

Making corrections: For now, as you are typing, use the following two keys to make corrections (See Figure 1-2 in Section 1): the *Backspace key* to delete characters to the left of the cursor and the *Del key* to delete characters at the cursor. WordPerfect also has an automatic insert mode. If you type new text, the characters to the right of your cursor will automatically move right.

Use the Enter key any time you see the paragraph marker (¶) in the letter.

Do not worry if your right margin wraps differently from the one shown in the example.

Press F1 if any messages appear in the status line or if you accidentally enter the wrong menu or screen. The F1 key is the Cancel key and will return you to your document.

```
(type today's date here)¶
¶
¶
¶
Patrick J. Pixby¶
32000 Randle Center, Suite 202¶
The Randle Scott Building¶
Seattle, WA 98101¶
¶
Dear Mr. Pixby:¶
¶
Thank you for your interest in the Wizzard's word
processing package.  Wizzard is easy to use yet
sophisticated.  It is not only a word processing package,
it is also a design tool, desktop publisher, and organizer
for your office.¶
¶
No matter what the size of your organization, the Wizzard
can handle your text typing needs.¶
¶
If you would like a demonstration of all of the Wizzard's
features, just give us a call.  Our number is on the
attached brochure.¶
¶
Sincerely,¶
¶
¶
¶
(Type your name here)¶
Vice President, Sales¶
¶
```

To Make Corrections

As you were typing the letter, you corrected errors with either the *Backspace* or *Del* keys. These keys are extremely useful for correcting errors immediately as you are typing the text or for correcting errors that are only a few characters in length. In this exercise, you will practice making several different kinds of corrections to the letter.

<u>The Backspace key and Ctrl Backspace</u>:

1. Press the **arrow keys** to move to the space prior to the word "easy" in the first paragraph

2. Press the **Backspace** key several times until the words "is" and "Wizzard" are removed

WATCH the screen as you are deleting the characters. Notice how the words to the right merge left with you as your cursor is moving left. If the word "Typeover" appears in the lower left of the screen, press the **insert** (Ins) key to shut it off. If the typeover feature remains on, each letter you type in the next step will replace a letter in the existing document.

3. Type **Wizzard is extremely** at the beginning of this sentence

WATCH as the characters to the right are automatically pushed to the right of the newly inserted text. NOTE: Some of the characters may be extending out from the right margin. If this happens, simply go to the next step and keep your eyes on the right margin.

4. Press the **Down Arrow** key to move down into your paragraph

When you press the down arrow key, any text extending out from the right margin is automatically aligned. This is called *automatic screen reformatting*.

5. Move your cursor to the **d** in the word "attached" in the last paragraph

6. Press **Ctrl Backspace** (hold down the Ctrl key, press the backspace key and then release both)

The entire word to the left of your cursor (attached) is deleted. This is a way of deleting more than just one character at a time. With just two keystrokes, you have deleted an entire word.

7. Type the word **enclosed** in front of "brochure" and watch as the text is moved right. Be sure to leave a space at the end.

8. Press the down arrow to align text if needed

The Typeover mode:

There is another way to make corrections quickly. Sometimes you do not want to push the text to the right of the cursor and would rather have the option of typing on top of the text, thus deleting it as you type.

1. Move to the **n** in the word "needs" at the end of paragraph two

2. Press the **Ins** key once

NOTE: The word Typeover appears in the lower left corner of your screen. You are now in Typeover mode.

3. Type the word **tasks** over "needs"

This time the word "needs" is not pushed to the right. It is replaced with the word "tasks."

4. Make any other corrections (if necessary) in your document until all spacing and spelling corrections have been made

To Save a Document

Now that you have a finished document on your screen, you should save it. There is one important step that should be completed prior to saving your document. You need to set the default drive to B (dual-disk system) or A (hard disk system). Do this step each time you sign onto WordPerfect or are ready to save your first file. It is best to do this step prior to retrieving a file from either B or A, since it cuts down on the number of steps used to retrieve a file.

To Set the Default Drive

If you were to save your file right now, you would save it with your WordPerfect program files since the automatic default is on A or C. It is always wise to keep the data files (document files) separate from the program or system files, and so the default drive must be changed.

<u>From a dual-disk or hard disk system</u>:

1. Press **F5**

A message appears in the lower right corner asking you to press the equals (=) sign to change the directory.

2. Press =

The A or C drive is shown (A:*.* or C:*.*).

3. Type **B:** (from a dual-disk system)

   or

   Type **A:** (from a hard disk system)

4. Press **Enter**

The new default directory prompt is now showing in the lower left corner of your screen (either B:*.* or A:*.*).

5. Press **F7** to return to your document

Your default drive is now set at B or A. For as long as you are working with WordPerfect during your current session (until you exit the program), you will not need to reset the drive. When you save a document now, it will automatically be stored on the disk in Drive B or A. You do, however, need to repeat these steps every time you sign onto the program from the A or C system prompt.

To Save

1. Press **F10**

2. Type **PIXBY** as the document name to be saved

3. Press **Enter**

The drive light on either B or A will flash briefly, and you may hear the sound of the drive as the document is being saved. When the process is finished, you are still in your document space.

This save command is good to use frequently as you are working on your document, particularly if you are working on a long, multi-page document. By using the F10 key as you are working, you are assured that if power is lost for any reason, your document will be safely stored on the diskette.

To Clear the Screen

Now that your document is finished, you would like to clear the screen so that you can begin a new one. Clearing the screen is done with the F7 or Exit key. Pressing the F7 key by itself (black lettering) has a dual purpose: clearing the screen or exiting the program. Both of these methods will be discussed here.

1. Press **F7**

A message appears asking whether you want to save your document. Anytime you press F7, this message will appear. It appears whether you are exiting the program or whether you just want to clear the screen. In this way, the program gives you the chance to save your document *before* you leave the program or clear the screen. If you did not have this option, you might exit or clear the screen and lose your unsaved document. The F7 key is therefore a second way of saving your document, the first being the F10 key. In general practice, use the F7 key as a secondary way of saving only if you forget to save before exiting the program or clearing the screen. Ordinarily, use the F10 key as the standard way of saving your document as you are working on it.

2. Type **N** for No to the message asking whether you want to save this document (it has already been saved so you do not need to save it again)

3. Type **N** for No again to the message asking whether you want to exit the program

Your screen is now blank.

NOTE: You must always clear the screen before retrieving a file from your B or A directory. If you do not, you will end up with both the document you just created and/or saved on the screen and the retrieved document on the screen.

To View the Directory

At this time, you might like to see what you have stored on your data disk in Drive B or A.

1. Press **F5**

Because the default drive was set, the drive name (B:*.* or A:*.*) appears in the lower left corner of your screen. This is the directory you want to look at, so

2. Press **Enter**

A directory similar to the one shown in Figure 2-2 appears.

```
04/31/90  10:20                  Directory B:\*.*
Document Size:        0                              Free Disk Space: 352299

. <CURRENT>  <DIR>                    | .. <PARENT>  <DIR>
PIXBY              98  04/31/90 9:34  |













1 Retrieve;  2 Delete;  3 Rename;  4 Print;  5 Text in;
6 Look;  7 Change Directory;  8 Copy;  9 Word Search;  0 Exit:  6
```

Figure 2-2. Directory of WordPerfect Data Files

As you can see from the figure, this screen is giving a lot of information. At the top of the screen, you will see the current date and time (if entered when first booting the system with DOS). The directory you are viewing is also shown on the first line. The second line shows the current document size and the free disk space remaining on your data disk. The name of the document you recently saved, PIXBY, is displayed. Notice that the PIXBY file has a period (.) after it. If you wanted, you could insert a three-character extension following the filename to categorize this file as a particular type of file, such as PIXBY.LTR for PIXBY letter. You do not need to type the extension, however, when saving the file.

To Retrieve a File

One of the choices at the bottom of the screen is for retrieving a file. Notice that a number appears opposite each choice: 1 for Retrieve, 2 for Delete, 3 for Rename, and so forth. To retrieve a file, you first use the arrow keys to highlight the filename. If you are unsure of the contents of the file, you can simply press Enter to view it. This is not a retrieval, however (you have not really loaded the file into memory), and so the file cannot be edited. To edit and load the file into memory, you must

1. Use the arrow keys to select the filename PIXBY

2. Press **1** to Retrieve PIXBY

You are returned to your screen with the PIXBY file retrieved.

NOTE: An A:\ or B:\ and the filename appear in the lower left corner of the screen.

To Exit without Saving

You will not make changes to this document now, so exit the program. Since it was saved correctly once, you can exit the program now without saving the document again. Remember, it is not lost; it is still saved on your diskette.

1. Press **F7**

2. Type **N** for No to the message asking whether you want to save the document

3. Type **Y** for Yes to the message asking whether you want to exit WordPerfect

You are returned to your system prompt, either A or C.

You should do the review questions next and then either continue or quit the program until the next session.

REVIEW QUESTIONS ON EXERCISE 2.2

1. Word wrap is

   a. text that automatically wraps to the next line regardless of the length of the line
   b. a fancy way to talk
   c. text that automatically moves to the next line when it will not fit within the right margin
   d. none of the above

2. The Del key deletes text at the cursor position

   a. a line at a time
   b. a character at a time
   c. a word at a time
   d. and also a character to the left

3. The Backspace key deletes text to the left of the cursor a character at a time.

   T F

4. What does the key combination Ctrl Backspace do?

5. You enter the Typeover mode by pressing:

   a. the Ins key
   b. the Enter key
   c. the Shift Backspace key combination
   d. the Ctrl Backspace key combination

6. The default drive is set by changing the directory through which of the following function keys?

   a. F10
   b. F2
   c. F3
   d. F5

7. It is necessary to press which of the following symbol keys to change the default drive (after pressing the correct function key)?

   a. +
   b. =
   c. /
   d. -

8. The quickest way to save your document on a regular basis is through which function key?

   a. F7
   b. F1
   c. F10
   d. the nearest one

9. The F7 key has which of the following multiple functions?

   a. Save and Exit
   b. Save and Clear the Screen
   c. Clear the Screen and Exit only
   d. Both a and b
   e. Both b and c

10. To see the current directory, you would press which key?

   a. F10
   b. F7
   c. F8
   d. F5

11. It is possible to retrieve a file from the directory into memory for editing by simply pressing the Return key.

   T F

Answers to the Review Questions on Exercise 2.2

1. c 2. b 3. T 4. Delete a word to the left of the cursor
5. a 6. d 7. b 8. c 9. d 10. d 11. F

EXERCISE 2.3. HOW TO PRINT A DOCUMENT

WordPerfect has many commands for printing a document. There are one or two, however, that are most commonly used and are the ones discussed in this exercise. Although the menus vary in appearance with WordPerfect 4.2 or WordPerfect 5.0, many of the numbers you press will be the same for both versions. The options in 4.2 usually appear at the bottom of your screen; those in 5.0 usually appear on a separate screen and are often itemized vertically on your screen.

Before you print your document, be sure you are online to the printer, the printer is turned on, and the paper is correctly aligned in the printer.

To Print a Full Document

One of the print commands that you will be using most often is the command to print your full document (all pages of the document). This is done with the Shift F7 combination of keys.

1. Load the program (if necessary)

2. First, retrieve the document from your B or A directory called PIXBY. (Use the F5 key and remember to set the default drive [change the directory] if you are just starting the computer.)

When the retrieved document is on your screen

3. Press **Shift F7** (hold the Shift key down and then press F7; release both)

Whether you are working with 4.2 or 5.0, you will see an option for the Full Document with the number 1 opposite it.

4. Press **1**

You will be returned to your document as it is printing.

NOTE: If you are using a student version, you will see *WPC printed throughout your document. This symbol is used as assurance that this limited version will not be applied to commercial uses.

To View a Document Prior to Printing

With WordPerfect, you also have the option of viewing your document exactly as it will print *prior* to printing it. Since this is a printing option, you find this command by using the Shift F7 key combination again.

1. Press **Shift F7**

2. Choose **6** (Print preview in 4.2 or View Document in 5.0)

NOTE to 5.0 users: When making the menu selections in 5.0 you have the option of using either the first or another character (shown in bold highlight) or pressing the number opposite the selection. In this guide, reference will be made to only the number used in the selection.

The document you now see on your screen is a small, basically unreadable form. What it does show is such elements as the placement of the address lines, the margins, and the spacing between paragraphs. The *View mode* is very useful when you are setting up headers or footers on a long document or when you have changed the margins and want to see the effect. Any time you are unsure of how the output will appear on the page, use the View mode. If necessary, you can return to the Edit mode and make changes prior to printing.

3. Press **1** for Document (in 4.2)

NOTE to 4.2 users: Your Preview mode looks very similar to your document; however, the true top and left margins are now displayed so that you can see exactly how the document will print on the page.

Options in View Mode

Some of the options you have in this mode are:

<u>in 4.2</u>:

Pressing 1 to preview the entire document or 2 to preview only the page where the cursor is resting (if the document is longer than this letter).

<u>in 5.0</u>:

Pressing 1, 2, or 3 to expand the document 100%, expand it 200%, or return to the full-page layout.

To Exit the View Mode

4. Press **F7** (the Exit key) to exit this mode

NOTE: The F7 key is used to exit, save changes made in menus, and return to the document.

Exit the program or continue.

REVIEW QUESTIONS ON EXERCISE 2.3

1. What combination of keys is used to reach the print options?

2. What option is used most often among the print options, and what number is pressed to reach this option?

3. How is the Print Preview or View Document mode reached?

4. How do you exit the View mode?

Answers to the Review Questions on Exercise 2.3

1. Shift F7 2. 1 for Full Document 3. Shift F7 and then option 6 4. F7 (the Exit function key)

INTERMEDIATE WORDPERFECT FUNCTIONS

PREVIEW

Among the functions used to make your document professional looking and your formatting easy is the ability to apply editing and formatting functions to your document. In this intermediate section, you will learn how to edit your PIXBY document, how to use the block command to manipulate large blocks of text, and how to change the line and page formatting as well as the format of characters in your document.

EXERCISE 2.4. HOW TO EDIT A DOCUMENT

There are many ways to edit your document in WordPerfect. You can add or delete lines, insert text, and merge paragraphs, to name only a few.

To Move through a Document

It is helpful to become comfortable with moving quickly through your document. So far, you have been moving through it with the use of the arrow keys. There are other, faster ways to get to another location in the document.

1. Retrieve the PIXBY document (if necessary)

Look at Figure 2-3. It shows how the cursor can be moved through your document. Practice some of these movements through this document.

When you press	The cursor moves
Right Arrow	one letter to the right
Left Arrow	one letter to the left
Up Arrow	up one line
Down Arrow	down one line
Ctrl/Right Arrow	one word to the right
Ctrl/Left Arrow	one word to the left
Home/Left Arrow	to the beginning of the current line
End/Right Arrow	to the beginning of the next line
End	to the end of the line
Home, Up Arrow	up one screen
Home, Down Arrow	down one screen
Pg Up	up one page
Pg Dn	down one page
Home, Home, Up Arrow	to the beginning of the document
Home, Home, Down Arrow	to the end of the document
Ctrl/Home, Up Arrow	to the beginning of a page
Ctrl/Home, Down Arrow	to the end of a page

Figure 2-3. Cursor Movement Keys

To Merge Paragraphs

Use this function to merge two paragraphs into one.

1. Position your cursor immediately after the period at the end of the first paragraph in the PIXBY document

2. Press the **Del** key twice so that the two paragraphs are merged into one

NOTE: Remember, the Del key deletes text at the cursor position. What just happened is that you deleted the two returns you had pressed at the end of the paragraph. Without the returns, the two paragraphs are not separated.

If your paragraphs are not joined after pressing the Del key twice, keep pressing Del until they are joined. Sometimes extra spaces can be added that are not visible on the screen. By continuing to press Del the paragraphs will eventually join.

3. Make sure "Typeover" doesn't appear at the lower left of the screen. If it does, press the **Ins** key to shut off Typeover.

4. Press the **Spacebar** so that two spaces appear between the two newly merged paragraphs

To Create Two Paragraphs

You can also create two paragraphs from one.

1. Position your cursor on the **N** of "No matter" at the beginning of the sentence you just merged (it might already be there)

2. Press the **Enter** key twice

Because of WordPerfect's automatic insert mode, the text from the cursor position and to the right of the cursor position will automatically be moved right (in this case down).

Good Job! Isn't that easy?

To Insert a Blank Line

You apply the same procedure used above to insert a blank line into your document. Suppose, for example, that you wanted to insert a blank line or two above the date line.

1. Move your cursor to the first character in the date line

2. Press **Enter** three times

Your entire document is moved down on the page. If you had moved to any other location in your document, the same would have occurred. Again, this is because of the automatic insert mode—anything from the cursor position to the right will be pushed forward or down.

To Save a Revised Document

Your document now has a few minor changes. You can quickly save the changes before continuing.

1. Press **F10**

The name of your document will appear at the bottom left of your screen.

2. Press **Enter**

3. Reply **Y** for Yes to replace the text

This command will replace the original version with the revised copy showing on your screen. As mentioned earlier in this section, it is wise to save the document you are working on at regular intervals. It is your insurance against losing all of your work.

EXERCISE 2.5. HOW TO BLOCK TEXT

You have learned how to use the Backspace, Del, and Ins keys to make corrections. There are other ways to make editing corrections to larger blocks of text. By using the *Copy* and *Move* commands you can make changes to large areas of text quickly. With the *block* functions, you use the Alt F4 key combination. This block key is used to highlight areas of text so that a function may be applied that will affect the entire block at once. With the Alt F4 keys you can block words, sentences, paragraphs, or entire documents.

To Move Blocked Text

1. Move to the blank line following your title, Vice President, Sales (Press **PgDn** once)

2. Press **Enter** twice to add two blank lines

3. Type the following paragraph (again, do not worry if the right margin aligns differently from the one shown here):

```
With the Wizzard, you can move or copy a block of text
to a new location in a document and repeat the command
one, two, three times, or more. You can also justify
text, center, add headings, and assign several fonts to
your document.  The Wizzard is your own desktop
publisher and editor.
```

4. Move your cursor to the W in "With" of the first line of this paragraph

5. Press **Alt F4**

NOTE: From now on it will be assumed that you will press the Alt (or other secondary key) first and then the function key; then, release both.

The words "Block On" flash in the lower left corner of your screen.

5. Press **Home, Home, Down Arrow** to move quickly to the end of your document (and thus the end of this paragraph)

The entire paragraph is now blocked.

With text blocked (such as this paragraph), you can do many things with it. For example, you could move it, delete it, copy it, or format it. Using the block command, you can also block any amount of text. Always apply the cursor movement keys to block text quickly once the block command is in effect.

6. Press **Ctrl F4**

This combination is the Move command. The Copy and Move functions are located in the same function key command.

7. Choose **1** to Cut Block (in 4.2)

   or

   Choose **1** or B for Block (in 5.0)

8. Choose **1** to Move (in 5.0)

You are now back in your document space and out of menus. Your next action is to move to the position where you want to insert the cut block of text.

9. Move the cursor to the space immediately after the period at the end of the second paragraph

10. Press the **spacebar** twice to add two spaces

11. (in 4.2 ONLY) Press **Ctrl F4** again

    Choose option **5** (Text)

    or

    (in 5.0 ONLY) Press **Enter** to insert the paragraph being moved

Your block of text is now inserted into its new location.

To Copy a Block of Text

Use the Copy command when you want to copy a block of text to a new location and leave it in its original location as well.

1. Block the third paragraph (hint: **Alt F4**). Use the **Down Arrow** to block.

2. Press **Ctrl F4** (the Move command is also used to copy)

3. (in 4.2) Choose **2** to Copy

   or

   (in 5.0) Choose **1** and then **2** to Copy Block

4. Position the cursor at the bottom of your document, two lines below your name

5. (in 4.2) Press **Ctrl F4** again and Choose **5** for text

   or

   (in 5.0) Press **Enter**

NOTE: If you had a block of text that you wanted to copy several times into various locations in your document, you would simply follow Steps 4 and 5 again and again until you had finished inserting all copies.

To Delete a Block of Text

Once text is blocked, you can also quickly Delete it. As you will see, this is much faster than repeatedly holding down the Del key or the Backspace key to remove text.

1. Move your cursor to the first character of the paragraph you just moved to the bottom of your document

2. Press **Alt F4**

3. Press **Home, Home, Down Arrow** to block to the end of the paragraph

4. Press the **Del** key

5. Press **Y** for Yes to delete the block

The paragraph is gone.

To Save and Retrieve a Block of Text

Sometimes you will want to save a frequently used block of text so that you can recall it for later use. In your current document, assume that you want to save the second paragraph describing the software you are selling. You frequently write paragraphs using the same wording and are tired of retyping them each time.

1. Move to the first character in the second paragraph

2. Block the paragraph

NOTE: Use a key combination other than **Home, Home, Down Arrow,** such as the **Down Arrow** key.

3. Press the **F10** key

NOTE: This key will save either the entire document or a block of text.

4. Type **FeaPara** for features paragraph to the message asking for a name for the block of text

5. Press **Enter**

The block of text is now saved as a separate file.

6. Save and replace your document now and clear the screen

Press: **F7**
Y to save the document
Enter
Y to save the revisions
Enter or **N** to exit the program

To Retrieve a Block of Text

You just saved a block of text under its own filename. It is permanently saved in your B or A directory (the diskette in either Drive B or Drive A) until you decide to delete it. You can now retrieve it into any document if you desire.

1. Press **Shift F10**

NOTE: This is a quick way to retrieve when you know the name of the file. It may be used for retrieving either a block of text or any one of the files in your directory.

2. Type **FeaPara** (the name of the stored block)

3. Press **Enter**

The paragraph is inserted into this document space.

NOTE: The paragraph was stored by blocking it and then saving it using the F10 function key. The blocking was done only to select specific text to be saved rather than saving the entire document. Whether you save a block of text or an entire document, to the program the result is the same—you are saving a file to disk.

To Restore Deleted Text

If you accidentally delete text that you wish you hadn't, you have an option in WordPerfect to restore the text. You must, however, remember to restore the text fairly soon after it has been deleted. After two deletions you cannot recover the text.

1. Move your cursor to the first character in your paragraph (it may be there now)

2. Press **Alt F4** to turn on block

3. Press **Home, Home, Down Arrow** to block the entire text

4. Press **Del** and **Y** to the message

Now,

5. Press the **F1** key (the Cancel key)

6. Choose **1** to restore (the blocked paragraph is showing on the screen) the recent deletion

The text magically reappears!

You may also have chosen 2 to restore the text after pressing F1. This would restore the previous deletion. One (1) restores the most recent deletion.

7. Clear your screen without saving by pressing **F7** and then pressing **N** for No two times

Continue to the Review Questions. Then exit the program or continue to Exercise 2.6.

REVIEW QUESTIONS ON EXERCISES 2.4 AND 2.5

1. State how you would quickly move the cursor in each of the following directions:

   one word to the right

   one word to the left

   to the beginning of the current line

   to the beginning of the document

2. State how two paragraphs are merged into one. How is one paragraph separated into two?

3. How do you save a revised copy of your document?

4. How do you move a block of text?

5. How do you copy a block of text?

6. How is a block of text deleted? How is it retrieved?

7. How is deleted text restored?

Answers to the Review Questions on Exercises 2.4 and 2.5

1. Ctrl, Right Arrow
   Ctrl, Left Arrow
   Home, Left Arrow
   Home, Home, Up Arrow

2. Merge by placing the cursor at the end of the first paragraph and pressing **Del** twice. Separate by placing the cursor on the first character of what will be the new paragraph and pressing **Enter** twice.
3. **F10, Enter, Y** to save the revision
4. in 4.2:
   Press **Alt F4** to block
   Press **Ctrl F4** (the Move/Copy command keys)
   Press **1**
   Position the cursor
   Press **Ctrl F4** again
   Choose **5** to insert text
   in 5.0:
   Press **Alt F4** to block
   Press **Ctrl F4** to move/copy
   Choose **1**
   Choose **1**
   Position the cursor
   Press **Enter**
5. in 4.2:
   Press **Alt F4** to block
   Press **Ctrl F4** to move/copy
   Choose **1**
   Position the cursor
   Press **Ctrl F4** again
   Choose **2**
   in 5.0:
   Press **Alt F4** to block
   Press **Ctrl F4** to move/copy
   Choose **1**
   Choose **2**
   Position cursor
   Press **Enter**
6. Press **Alt F4** to block
   Press **Del**
   to restore
   Press **F1** to cancel
   Choose **1** to undelete or **2** to restore previous deletion
7. **F1**
   2

EXERCISE 2.6. HOW TO FORMAT PAGES

You have learned several basic methods of editing your text. Now it is time to learn how to make the text look professional and distinctive through the use of WordPerfect's formatting features.

1. Type the document shown on the following page. Do not worry about where the right margin wraps. As with other exercises in this guide, the right margin may align differently from the one shown.

2. When finished, check for errors in the document and make any corrections. Save the document as REPORT. If you are just signing on, be sure to change your directory to B or A (set the default drive).

```
DEMAND FOR QUALIFIED DATA PROCESSING PERSONNEL
Study Developed by the Human Resources Department
SeaTech Corporation


Background

As the area of data processing in the business community
grows, the demand for qualified personnel also soars in our
industry.  SeaTech has increased in size by 100 percent over
the last five years, and the need to fill an ever increasing
number of data processing vacancies is serious.

As employers, however, we need to differentiate between
potentially good employees and effective data processing
employees.  Developing the basic criteria to define a
"qualified programmer" for instance, starts with fundamental
education background.  In prior years, the criteria was
equipment operation skills.  As the field has expanded and
the work become extremely technical, business management has
begun to reevaluate the staffing needs of its data processing
and MIS departments.

The basic skills needed to write programs for SeaTech cannot
be learned on the job.  Those skills must come through an
accredited institution offering courses in computer science,
software applications, and programming skills.
```

To Change the Line Spacing

Now that you have finished the basic document, you have decided that it needs to be in proper report format, and thus needs to be double spaced. This is easy to do with WordPerfect's format options.

Spacing can be changed for the entire document quickly and easily without blocking text. If, however, you wish to change only portions of the document to double space, you need to block those portions. For now, practice double spacing the entire document including the heading.

1. Move to the first character at the top of the page (the D in DEMAND)

Here the instructions for 4.2 and 5.0 will vary and so will be listed separately.

in 4.2:

These steps are displayed at the bottom of your screen and are fairly easy to follow.

2. Press **Shift F8**

3. Choose **4** to access the spacing options

4. Type **2** as the number of line spaces you want (for double spacing)

5. Press **Enter**

in 5.0:

These steps are displayed in a series of main and submenu options shown below.

2. Press **Shift F8**

You will see a list of formatting options on the full screen as shown in Figure 2-4.

```
Format

     1 - Line
          Hyphenation                    Line Spacing
          Justification                  Margins Left/Right
          Line Height                    Tab Set
          Line Numbering                 Widow/Orphan Protection

     2 - Page
          Center Page (top to bottom)    New Page Number
          Force Odd/Even Page            Page Numbering
          Headers and Footers            Paper Size/Type
          Margins Top/Bottom             Suppress

     3 - Document
          Display Pitch                  Redline Method
          Initial Codes/Font             Summary

     4 - Other
          Advance                        Overstrike
          Conditional End of Page        Printer
          Decimal Characters             Underline
          Language

Selection: 0
```

Figure 2-4. The Format Menu in 5.0

Among those options are Line (or 1) options.

3. Choose **1** for the line options

You have moved to the line submenu shown in Figure 2-5.

Format: Line

1 - Hyphenation	Off
2 - Hyphenation Zone - Left	10%
- Right	4 %
3 - Justification	Yes
4 - Line Height	Auto
5 - Line Numbering	No
6 - Line Spacing	1
7 - Margins - Left	1"
- Right	1"
8 - Tabs Set	0", every 0.5"
9 - Widow/Orphan Protection	No

Selection: 0

Figure 2-5. The Format: Line Menu in 5.0

4. Choose **6** to move to the space after Option 6

5. Type **2** for double spacing

6. Press **F7** twice to return to your document

NOTE: Pressing the F7 key in Step 6 is very important. It saves the changes just made. Any time you enter a menu and make formatting or other changes, always use the F7 key to return to your document space. It is essential in saving the new changes.

<u>to both 4.2 and 5.0 users:</u>

Your document is now double spaced.

To Create Hanging Indents

A hanging indent is text that automatically wraps to an indented point on the left margin rather than returning to the left margin. It usually begins with the second line of typed text in a paragraph or with itemized numbers. Look, for instance, at instruction number 2 immediately below. Notice that the number 2 is on the left margin and the instruction begins one tab width to the right of the number. Then the instruction line hits the right margin and wraps to the indent (not to the left margin). This is an example of a hanging indent. Hanging indents are done by pressing the F4 key to move the cursor to the tab where the indent will occur instead of pressing the regular Tab key.

1. Move to the bottom of your document

2. Press **Enter** twice to move to a new blank line and to leave one blank line after your last paragraph

3. Type the first sentence of the text shown in the box on the following page. Press **Enter** twice after the word "are."

4. Type **1**. at the left margin

5. Press **F4** instead of the Tab key to move to the 1.5 default tab setting. Type the first sentence after 1 without pressing Enter at the right margin.

6. Press **Enter** once after each item. Continue to type the remaining items using the **F4 key** each time to tab after typing the number.

NOTE: The default tabs are set every .5 inch.

```
The criteria on which we need to place an emphasis for
new industry recruits are:

1.    The qualified applicant should possess skills in
      fundamental computer concepts and terminology.
2.    The qualified applicant should possess at least a
      two-year degree in computer science, business, or a
      related field.
3.    He/she should have a working knowledge of COBOL as
      well as three software application programs,
      including a word processing program, a spreadsheet
      program, and a database program.
4.    He/she should have excellent written and oral
      communication skills.
```

7. Save your document as REPORT (**F10**).

To Change the Tab Settings

You have learned that the default tab settings are every .5 inch. There may be many reasons that you want to change the tab settings. If you want to add columns of figures to this document, for example, it would be awkward to press the Tab key 5 times to move toward the center of your page. It would be very convenient, however, to have only the necessary tab stops on your page so that pressing the Tab key once would send you to the correct location.

1. Move your cursor to the bottom of your document and press the **Enter** key twice

2. Type the short paragraph shown in the box on the next page. Press **Enter** twice at the end of the paragraph.

```
At present, we have the following openings.  The criteria
stated should be given priority in placement for these
positions:

            Data Entry                          6.50/hr
            Data Processing Asst. 1             7.00
            Data Processing Asst. 2             7.50
            Data Processing Senior Rep.         8.00
            Programmer 1                        8.00
            Programmer 2                       10.00
```

3. Press **Shift F8** (in both 4.2 and 5.0)

4. Choose **1** (in both 4.2 and 5.0)

5. Choose **8** (in 5.0 ONLY)

The ruler line is displayed at the bottom of your screen as shown in Figure 2-6.

```
L....  .L......L.......L.....  L.......L......  L....  ..L....  ..L.......L.......L......L....  .L.......L....  .L.......L...
12345678901234567890123456789012345678901234567890123456789012345678901234567890123456789012345678
          20          30          40          50          60          70          80
Delete EOL (clear tabs);  Enter number (set tab);  Del (clear tab);
Left;  Center;  Right;  Decimal;  .= Dot leader;  press EXIT when done.
```

Figure 2-6. The Tab Screen

This ruler line shows all of the default tabs (L for left align at every .5 inch). It also counts the number of spaces from 0 to 9 between the tab positions and shows the total number of spaces across the entire width of the paper (e.g., 20, 30, 40, 50, through 80).

<u>in both 4.2 and 5.0</u>:

6. Press **Ctrl End** to delete all of the tab settings

7. Use your **Right Arrow** key to move to 2.5 (halfway between 20 and 30) on the ruler line

8. Press **L** for a left-aligned tab setting at 2.5

9. Move to **6.0** on the ruler line

10. Press **D** for a decimal tab setting

NOTE: Later when you tab to 6.0 and the decimal tab setting, your decimal points will automatically align.

11. Press the **F7** key once in 4.2 and twice in 5.0 to return to your document

Your tabs are now correctly set.

12. Type the remainder of the two columns in the table. As you type, tab once to the first column, type it, then tab to the second column and type it without spacing. When you press the period, the decimal will automatically align at the tab stop.

To Change the Table to Single Spacing

Change the table to single spacing.

1. Move to the line above the first line in the table

2. Press **Shift F8** (in both 4.2 and 5.0)

3. Choose **4** (in 4.2)

   or

   Choose **1** and then **6** (in 5.0)

4. Type **1** to change to single spacing

5. Press **Enter** (in 4.2)

   or

   Press **F7** twice (in 5.0)

The text in the table is single spaced.

NOTE: The spacing will take effect from the position of the cursor downward in the document.

To Center a Line

There are several things left that would make this document look even better than it already does. One is to center the headings at the top of the document. In this case, the line is already typed, so you will need to block the line(s) to be centered.

1. Move your cursor to the **D** in DEMAND of the main heading

2. Press **Alt F4** to turn on the block mode

3. Press **End** to block to the end of the line

4. Press **Shift F6** to center the line (note the word "Center" in green on your template)

5. Press **Y** for Yes to center

6. Center both the second and third line headings

NOTE: To make the process go faster, block both lines at once. If you had not already typed the text and wanted to center a heading prior to typing it, you would press **Shift F6** and then type the heading, press **Enter**, and press **Shift F6** again to turn off the Center mode.

7. Save your revised document and clear the screen or quit

Continue to the Review Questions.

REVIEW QUESTIONS ON EXERCISE 2.6

1. List the steps necessary to change the line spacing in a document.

2. What key is used in place of the Tab key to create a hanging indent?

3. How do you delete all tab settings? How are new tabs set?

4. How is a line centered on the page?

Answers to the Review Questions on Exercise 2.6

1. Press **Shift F8** (in 4.2)
   Choose **4**
   Type the number for the spacing
   Press **Enter**

   or

   Press **Shift F8** (in 5.0)
   Choose **1** and then **6**
   Type the number for the spacing
   Press **F7** twice
2. **F4**
3. After pressing **Shift F8** (in 4.2 and 5.0)
   (with 4.2 press **1** after **Shift F8**)
   Press **Ctrl End** to delete all tab settings
   Press the correct letter at the correct location on the ruler line to set new tabs (such as D for decimal; L for left align, etc.)
4. **Shift F6**

EXERCISE 2.7. HOW TO FORMAT CHARACTERS

Character formatting applies special characteristics to the individual characters in your text, such as a word that is underlined, or characters that appear in bold print or in different fonts.

To Make Text Bold

1. Retrieve the document called REPORT

2. Move to the **D** in DEMAND of the centered heading at the top of the page

3. Block the line with **Alt F4** and **End**

4. Press **F6** (Note the black letter on the F6 key and the word "Bold")

NOTE: In the lower right corner of your screen the Pos indicator figure is in bold print. This is one of the functions of the Pos indicator—it shows the location of various formats in your document.

5. Press the **Down Arrow** (Pos is no longer showing in bold and the block turns off automatically)

To Underline Text

1. Block the word "Background" prior to the first paragraph

2. Press **F8** for underline

NOTE: The word changes to a shaded background. This is the way underlined text appears on the screen. Notice that Pos in the lower right side of the screen is also shaded.

To Format Characters Prior to Typing

You have the option of either assigning special character formats either prior to or after typing text (as discussed earlier). To assign formats prior to typing the text, do the following:

1. Move your cursor to the **p** in "priority" in the sentence prior to the table

2. Press **F6** for bold

3. Type **first**

4. Press **F6** to turn off bold

5. Press the **spacebar** once

To Change the Font and Point Size

If your printer has the capability, you will be able to change the font size and point size so that your text takes on a really personal appearance and professional characteristics. Changing the fonts and points gives the document qualities of what is called *desktop publishing*. In other words, it looks publishable.

1.	Move to the first line of your heading again	
2.	Press **Ctrl F8**	(in both 4.2 and 5.0)
3.	Choose **1**	(in 4.2)
	or	
	Choose **4**	(in 5.0)
4.	Enter the Pitch Number (such as 14)	(in 4.2 only)
	Press **Enter**	

Enter the Font Number (Type 5) (in 4.2 only)

NOTE: Enter a number like 14 for the pitch and the number 5 for the font number (or any other number if not available).

or

Select **Roman 12 CPI** by pressing **1** to make the selection (in 5.0)

(Or pick any other available font different from Courier 10)

5. Press **Enter** and then **F7** (in 4.2 only)

or

Press **F7** once (in 5.0)

The heading still appears in bold print, centered. When you print, the new font will appear.

6. Save the revised document and quit now or continue to the Review Questions and the next exercise.

REVIEW QUESTIONS ON EXERCISE 2.7

1. How do you make text bold after it has been typed?

2. What key is used to underline text?

3. How are the font and point sizes changed?

4. How is text underlined prior to typing?

Answers to the Review Questions on Exercise 2.7

1. Block it, then press the format key **F6**
2. F8
3. See the complete instructions on the previous pages.

4. Press **F8**, type the text, then press **F8** again to turn off the underline mode

EXERCISE 2.8. HOW TO USE REVEAL CODES

Reveal Codes are an integral part of using WordPerfect. You must enter Reveal Codes to be certain of editing changes you have made in your document. Often what you have done with your document and what shows on the screen may be entirely different from what will actually print. If this is the case, what is really taking place in your document can be discovered in Reveal Codes. They should be referred to frequently as an accurate picture of what is really occurring in your document formatting.

1. Retrieve the document called REPORT (if necessary)

2. Move to the **A** of At in the line above the table

3. Press **Alt F3** (for Reveal Codes)

Your screen splits in two parts. The top half is the same (showing your document); the bottom half is in Reveal Codes and shows all of the keys you have pressed, text you have typed, and special formats you have given. It looks approximately like the one shown in Figure 2-7.

```
At present, we have the following openings.  The criteria stated
should be given priority in placement for these positions:

                Data Entry                        $ 6.50/hr
                Data Processing Asst. 1             7.00
                Data Processing Asst. 2             7.50
                Data Processing Senior Rep.         8.00
                Programmer 1                        8.00
C:\WP4.2\DATA\SECTION2                     Doc 1 Pg 1  Ln 2.5" Pos 1"
[   ^     ^     ^     ^     ^                              ]
At present, we have the following openings.  The criteria stated[SRt]
should be given priority in placement for these positions:[HRt]
[Font:*Courier 10 pitch (Roman-8)[HRt]
[HRt]
[Tab Set:0",2.5",6"][Tab]Data Entry[Align]$ 6[C/A/Flrt].50/hr[HRt]
[Tab]Data Processing Asst. 1[Align]7[C/A/Flrt].00[HRt]
[Tab]Data Processing Asst. 2[Align]7[C/A/Flrt].50[HRt]
[Tab]Data Processing Senior Rep.[Align]8[C/A/Flrt].00[HRt]
[Tab]Programmer 1[Align]8[C/A/Flrt].00[HRt]
[Tab]Programmer 2[Align]10[C/A/Flrt].00[HRt]

Press Reveal Codes to restore screen
```

Figure 2-7. Reveal Codes

The codes showing in the bottom half of your screen represent all of the keys you have pressed and the special formats you have assigned. Look closely at the screen. Some of the codes visible on your screen now are:

[SRt] — indicating a soft return or the automatic word wrap

[HRt] — indicating places where you have pressed the Enter key or a hard return

[Font:*Courier 10 pitch...

indicating what font is in use

[Tab] — indicating that you pressed the Tab key at this location

[Align] — indicating where a decimal align tab was pressed

As you work with Reveal Codes, you will learn to read the codes and understand their meanings, especially since you will remember that you used a decimal tab at a certain location or changed the font at another location. If there are codes that you do not understand or that you think should not be there, you can delete them.

To Delete in Reveal Codes

You can add text or delete codes and text in Reveal Codes just as you would when not in Reveal Codes. Deleting in Reveal Codes is perhaps easiest when you are deleting a format such as a center or bold format.

1. Move to the top of your document while still in Reveal Codes (Press **Home, Home, Up Arrow**)

2. Look in Reveal Codes to locate the center command used to center the first line heading

   It should contain the following codes in a similar format:

[C][Font change:14,5][B][Spacing Set:2]DEMAND FOR QUALIFIED DATA PROCESSING PERSONNEL[b][c][HRt]

The large [C] at the beginning of the line denotes where the center command was given. The small [c] at the end of the line shows where the command ends. When you center a line, the large and small C's are inserted by the program automatically. You can delete the center code by deleting the large [C]. The small [c] will be deleted at the same instant. The large and small B's ([B][b]) indicate a bold command. You also see the command for changing the font.

NOTE: This font size will remain in effect for the entire document unless you change it back to the regular font after the heading line.

3. Move your cursor to the space just prior to the large [C] before the heading

NOTE: In Reveal Codes, your cursor will always take up a space even though it appears under a character in regular edit mode.

4. Press **Del**

The centering is gone.

5. To center the line again while in Reveal Codes, **block** it and press **Shift F6** twice. The line will center and the [C] and [c] will be reinserted.

You will automatically leave Reveal Codes as soon as you give a formatting command. Repeating Alt F3 will also remove the Reveal Codes screen.

ADVANCED WORDPERFECT FUNCTIONS

PREVIEW

In the following advanced WordPerfect functions exercises, you will polish your word processing skills. There are many advanced features to this program. Some of the more frequently used ones will be discussed here, such as creating headers or footers, which will appear on every page of a document, after typing it only one time; printing selected pages of a long document or printing multiple copies; searching for text and replacing text; and running a spell check.

EXERCISE 2.9. HOW TO CREATE HEADERS OR FOOTERS AND NUMBER PAGES ON A LONG DOCUMENT

Headers and footers are one or more lines of text that appear at the top or bottom of your document, respectively. They are often used in books or manuscripts to identify a chapter, section, or title of a project. The headings at the top of the pages in this book are an example of headers. WordPerfect has the ability to create headers and/or footers at the top of every page, every odd page, or every even page.

Usually headers and footers are a few lines in length. You could create one that is several lines long, but usually this is not practical since that would leave little room on the page for the rest of your text. You can also create headers and footers that face each other on facing, or opposite, pages (again, this book is an example of that type of design). You can see the placement of a header or footer by looking in Reveal Codes.

To Create a Header

1. Retrieve the document called REPORT (if necessary)

2. Move the cursor to the very top of the document (so that it is under the first character of your first heading)

3. Press **Alt F8** (in 4.2)

   or

   Press **Shift F8** (in 5.0)

4. Choose **6** (in 4.2)

or

Choose **2** for Page
and then **3** for Headers (in 5.0)

5. Type **1** for the header number (in 4.2)
and then **1** for Every Page

or

Choose **1** for Header
and then **2** for Every Page (in 5.0)

You are in a blank screen now that looks similar to your document screen. This is the screen for typing and saving a header.

6. Type the following text as the heading:

```
^N / Data Processing Report, 1990
```

NOTE: The ^N is created by pressing **Shift 6** and a capital **N.** This instruction will insert a page number at that location when the document is printed.

8. Press **F7** to exit (in both 4.2 and 5.0)
and save the header and
Press **F7** again

9. Save the revised document

At this time you may view the document (**Shift F7**) to see the headers in place. (Press **F7** to exit View mode.)

To Print Selected Pages of a Long Document

You have used the F7 key before by pressing the Shift F7 key combination to print the full document. Suppose you wanted to print only the second page of your document. In that case, you would:

with 4.2:

1. Position the cursor anywhere in Page 2

2. Press **Shift F7**

3. Choose **2** to send the page to the printer

The page on which your cursor is located will print.

NEXT, try the second method of printing selected pages. This command is used to print either a single page or a range of pages.

1. Position the cursor on any page in your document

2. Press **Shift F7**

3. Choose **4** for Printer Control

4. Choose **P** for Print a Document

You'll see a menu for typing the document name in the middle of your screen, so

5. Type the document name, REPORT

6. Press **Enter**

To print selected pages, type

7. **2** for the second page

8. Press **F7** to return to your document

<u>with 5.0:</u>

1. Position your cursor anywhere in the document

2. Press **Shift F7**

3. Choose **3** for document on disk

4. Type the document name: **REPORT**

5. Press **Enter**

6. Type the range of pages: **2**

7. Press **Enter**

8. Press **F7** to return to your document

The document is printing.

NOTE to users of both 5.0 and 4.2: You could enter a range to print of any number of combinations, such as: 5-11, 18, 21-24 as one range, or 6-11, 15, 21 as another range of pages.

To Control the Printer

You can display all of the print jobs that are stacked up for printing. Using the same command you can also stop a print job.

1. Press **Shift F7** (in both 4.2 and 5.0)

2. Choose **4** to Control the Printer

If a job is printing, it will appear in the Job List section of the screen. You can cancel a job by pressing C for Cancel Print Job(s), press R for a rush job that will be done before other jobs are completed, press D to display all print jobs, or press S to stop the printer, and G to make the printer go again after a stop command.

3. At this time, press **F7** to return to your document

To Print from List Files

You can print with the F5 (List Files) function key as well as with the Shift F7 key. Most of the time you will probably print with Shift F7, but if you are certain of the appearance of your stored document, it is convenient to print directly from List Files.

1. Press **F5** for List Files

2. Press **Enter** to view your current directory (B or A)

3. Choose **PIXBY**

4. Choose **4** to print the document

The document is printing.

5. Press **F7** to return to your document, REPORT

6. Clear your screen now, and either Exit or continue to the next section.

EXERCISE 2.10. HOW TO SEARCH FOR AND/OR REPLACE TEXT

You can search for particular words in your document. You can also search for text and replace it with other text. If a date, for example, is entered many times throughout a long document, you can quickly change the date by searching for the original entry and replacing it with the new date. This can be done in a single command so that in a long document all dates are replaced in one step.

With WordPerfect, you can search for as many as 59 characters at a time. Using the search option is also often the fastest way to move through a very long document to reach a specific section. You can do this by searching for a particular word or group of words in an area of a document, such as a chapter heading or other titles appearing on the page.

To Search for Text

1. Retrieve the document, REPORT (if necessary)

2. Move your cursor to the beginning of your document

3. Press **F2** (the Forward Search key)

The cursor now appears to the right of your Srch; the prompt is in the lower left corner of the screen.

4. Type **data** as the word for which you are searching

5. Press **F2** again to start the search process

NOTE: DO NOT press the Enter key this time. If you do, you will see the HRt code that is also visible in Reveal Codes. You begin and end a search process using the Search (F2) key.

At this time, you could edit the word "data" or add text at this location in your document. Leave the word as is for now.

To Repeat the Search

You can find other occurrences of the word "data" throughout the text. If you entered the word at the beginning of the search process in lowercase letters, Search will locate all occurrences of data in both upper- or lowercase. If you had entered data in uppercase letters, however, Search would locate only the word "Data" in uppercase letters.

To Continue Searching for "Data"

1. Press **F2** again (the word "data" is still there) to begin the search

2. Keep pressing **F2** until all occurrences are found and the *Not found* prompt appears

You can press the F1 key at any time to cancel the search. You can also search forward or backward in your document using the following process:

1. Press **F2**

2. Type the word for which you are searching

3. Press the **Up Arrow** to search backward in your document

4. Press the **Down Arrow** to switch to forward searching

To Replace Text

You can quickly search for and replace existing text with this command. Do the following:

1. Move to the beginning of your document

2. Press **Alt F2** for the Replace command

3. Press **Y** for Yes to confirm each replacement

NOTE: Pressing N for No would replace for every occurrence automatically without your confirmation.

4. Type **data processing** in lowercase letters

5. Press **F2**

6. Type **MIS computer** in response to the "replace with" message

7. Press **F2**

You'll see a "Please wait" message, and then the question:

Confirm? (Y/N) No

to the first occurrence of "data processing."

7. Press **Y** for Yes to each occurrence of "data processing" until the confirm message no longer appears and all occurrences are located

8. Save the document, replacing the previous version

9. Clear the screen

REVIEW QUESTIONS ON EXERCISES 2.9 AND 2.10

1. In both 4.2 and 5.0, headers are created using which function key in conjunction with the Shift key?

   a. F6
   b. F5
   c. F7
   d. F8

2. List all of the steps used to create a header.

3. Which number is chosen after pressing Shift F7 to print selected pages of a long document?

4. How do you print from List Files?

5. Which is the correct sequence of keystrokes used when searching for text?

   a. F2, type the search word, F2 again
   b. F2, type the search word, Enter
   c. F2, type the search word, Ctrl F2
   d. none of the above

6. To continue the search process, which function key do you press?

7. Which is the correct key combination used to replace text?

   a. Shift F2
   b. Shift F1
   c. Alt F2
   d. Alt F1

Answers to the Review Questions on Exercises 2.9 and 2.10

2.	Press **Shift F8**	(in both 4.2 and 5.0)
	Choose **6**	(in 4.2)
	or	
	Choose **2** for Page	(in 5.0)
	Type **1** for the header number	(in 4.2)
	or	
	Choose **1** for Header	
	and then **2** for Every Page	(in 5.0)
	Type the following heading	
	Press **F7** in 4.2 and 5.0	
3.	in 4.2: Choose **2**	
	in 5.0: Choose **3**	
4.	Press **F5**, highlight the filename, press **4** to print	
5.	a	
6.	F2 again	
7.	c	

EXERCISE 2.11. HOW TO CHECK SPELLING AND USE THE THESAURUS

To Run a Spelling Check

A spelling checker, or speller, enables you to check each word in your document for correct spelling. It is a feature that can be quite useful, especially if you have problems spelling. The speller that is available with the full-featured version of WordPerfect contains over 115,000 words and lets you add new words as you need them. The educational version has far fewer words, and it can only show in a very limited way how the spelling-checker feature works. If you are using the educational version, realize its limitations and focus on the concept of the spelling checker.

Type the following text with all of the spelling errors:

```
"In order to praticipate in the game of litarature, you not
only have to know the rules of the langwage, but also the
precise but also the precise but flexible ruels of
leterature itself.  Each of the forms of literature
impposses its own set of rules.  A sonnnet must be fourteen
lines, for exampal, and a storey should give some kind of
resulution to its complicasions and conflicts.  These rules
are more flexable than the the ruels of language."

     Thomas McLaughlin, The Power of Literature
```

The way you begin your spelling check depends on the version of WordPerfect you are using. In the full-featured version, the speller is shown on its disk; in the educational version, the speller is on the disk with the WordPerfect program. If you are using a hard disk system with the full-featured or student versions, the speller will be contained with the program on the hard disk.

In any version of the program,

1. Press **Ctrl F2**

In the educational version, you will be ready to go on to Step 2. You can also continue if using a hard disk system. Those of you who might be using a full version with a dual-disk system should follow the directions on your screen for removing the data disk and inserting the speller.

When ready, a message will appear on the screen that says:

1 Enter Path 2 Skip Language 3 Exit

The following message appears:

1 Word; 2 Page; 3 Document; 4 New Supplemental Dictionary; 5 Lookup; 6 Cc

2. Choose **3** for the Entire Document

NOTE: Pressing F1 at any time will end the spell-check operation.

At this time a screen similar to the one in Figure 2-8 appears.

"In order to praticipate in the game of litarature, you not only have to know the rules of the langwage, but also the precise but also the precise but flexible ruels of leterature itself. Each of the forms of literature imposses its own set of rules. A sonnnet must be fourteen lines, for exampal, and a storey should give some kind of resulution to its complicasions and conflicts. These rules are more flexable than the the ruels of language."

Thomas McLaughlin, <u>The Power of Literature</u>

===

A. participate

Not Found: 1 Skip Once; 2 Skip; 3 Add; 4 Edit; 5 Look Up; 6 Ignore Numbers;0

Figure 2-8. Spell Check Screen

Incorrect words are highlighted. If the dictionary contains more than one word that might be the misspelled word, a list of possible correct words is shown in the lower half of the screen.

Options you have at this time are listed at the bottom of the screen.

<u>Selecting 1</u> would skip this misspelled word at this time, without making corrections, but will catch it if it appears later in the document.

<u>Selecting 2</u> will skip the selected word at this time and for the remainder of the document.

<u>Selecting 3</u> will add the word to the dictionary, assuming it is correctly spelled but is not in WordPerfect's dictionary.

<u>Selecting 4</u> will allow you to return to your document to edit the word or correct it from the keyboard. After you have corrected the word, pressing F7 will return you to the spelling check.

<u>Selecting 5</u> will allow you to check on specific word patterns of your choice.

When the list of suggested words is displayed, you press the letter of the correct spelling. The word will be corrected, and the next misspelled word is located.

To Correct Double Words

When double words occur such as "the the" in the last line of your paragraph, you will see the following message:

1 2 Skip; 3 Delete 2nd; 4 Edit; 5 Disable Double Word Checking

Usually you will want to select 3 to delete the second word. Selecting 5 will discontinue the check.

3. Correct the spelling of the paragraph using the discussed procedures.

4. Save a copy of the paragraph as SPELL.

PRACTICE DOCUMENTS

NOTE TO THE STUDENT

These exercises cover many of the WordPerfect features presented in this guide. There are four documents presented here. Completing each of them as outlined in the instructions will reinforce most of the functions in this guide so that you will be able to use and recall them for future use without continual reference to the guide.

PRACTICE DOCUMENT 1: A LETTER

Objectives:

In this exercise you will practice:

a. the Center command
b. the Underline command
c. clearing and setting tabs
d. using the Typeover mode
e. making corrections
f. printing

1. Clear all tab settings
2. Set a tab at approximately .5 inch to the right of center on the ruler line. Use this setting for the date and closing
3. Begin typing the letter on the following page. Use four hard returns after the date
4. Single space the entire letter. However, double space between the city and salutation, the salutation and the first paragraph, the first and second paragraph, and prior to "Yours very truly."
5. Use four hard returns between the closing line (Yours very truly) and the author's name, J. T. College

NOTE: Don't worry if the lines of text do not wrap exactly as shown in the letter. Let Word Wrap hit the right margin and wrap where it will.

```
                                   (Type today's date)



Florence L. Smythe
SeaTech Corporation
East Coast Division
30 Industrial Avenue
Pittsburgh, PA 15230

Dear Ms. Smythe:

I certainly enjoyed my visit to SeaTech Corporation and the
lively talk we had over lunch.  Of course, I am still very
interested in the opening in your accounting department, and I
will notify you of my employment decision as soon as my last
interview is finished next month.

Enclosed is a copy of a recent curriculum vitae.  I apologize
for not having a copy to give you during my visit.


                                   Yours very truly,



                                   J. T. College
```

6. Save the letter on disk as SMYTHE
7. Print a copy of the letter
8. Use the List Files command to make sure your document has been saved on your data disk
9. Make the following changes to the second paragraph:

    a. insert the words: **are two copies** after the word "Enclosed"
    b. delete the words: **is a copy** in the same sentence
    c. insert the word: **sincerely**, between "I" and "apologize" in the next sentence
    d. change the words: **a copy** in the same sentence to the word: **one**

10. Save a copy of the revisions under the same name
11. Print a copy of the revised letter
12. Insert the following paragraph as the second paragraph in the letter

```
Enclosed also is a list of expenses I
incurred on the trip.  I would appreciate
your reimbursing me at your earliest
possible convenience.
```

13. Move the paragraph just typed so that it is the third instead of the second paragraph
14. Save the letter again under the same name
15. Print a final and third copy of the letter
16. Clear your screen

NOTES

PRACTICE DOCUMENT 2: A TABLE

<u>Objectives</u>:

In this exercise you will practice:

a. clearing and setting tabs
b. setting dot leaders
c. creating hanging indents
d. character formatting text
e. using the Block command
f. using the Restore feature
g. using double underline

Type the document shown in the box using the following guidelines:

1. Type the **three lines of the heading** as shown. Press **two hard returns** after the third heading line.

```
                 EXPENSES SUMMARY
                  J. T. COLLEGE
         Visit to SeaTech Corporation, date

1. Airfare ..............................$300.00
2. Hotel ................................  90.00
3. Meals ................................  65.00

   Total ................................$455.00

Notes:

1. The airfare consisted of a round-trip coach ticket
from San Francisco.  I have enclosed a copy of the
receipt with this letter.
2. Receipt also enclosed.
3. I lost the meal receipts, but, since meals are being
billed to my credit card, I can get receipts if you need
them.
```

2. Clear all tabs
3. Set new tabs as follows:

a left-aligned tab at 1.5 inches
a decimal tab at approximately 6.0
a dot leader tab at 5.5 (press a period at 5.5 on the ruler line)

NOTE: Remember to exit with F7 so that the tab settings are saved.

4. Type the **itemized list** using the following guidelines:

   a. type the **1.**
   b. press the **Tab** key
   c. type **Airfare**
   d. press the **Tab** key (the dots will appear)
   e. press the **Tab** key again to move to the decimal tab position
   f. type the number, **$300.00**
   g. press **Enter**

   Repeat for the first three lines of the table and the "Total" line. Leave a blank line before total.

5. Press **Return** twice after the "Total" line
6. Type **Notes,** underscored
7. When typing the itemized numbers under Notes, be sure to press **F4 instead of the Tab key.** You do not need to change any other tab settings.
8. Block and delete **Number 3** of Notes
9. Restore **Number 3** with the **F1** key
10. Use Reveal Codes to inspect the codes, and, while in Reveal Codes, add the following features:

    a. make the first line of the heading bold
    b. underline 65.00 in the decimal tab column
    c. underline the total figure: $455.00

11. Double space the **Notes** text
12. Proof the document and save it as EXPENSES
13. Print a copy of the document
14. Clear the screen

PRACTICE DOCUMENT 3: A REPORT

Objectives:

The objectives of this exercise are to:

a. use the Underline feature
b. use the Center feature
c. create a header
d. change line spacing
e. run a spelling check
f. change the right margin to a ragged right margin
g. save and print a multi-page document

1. Type the following document as shown. Do not worry about how the right margin wraps but DO type the misspelled words as shown.
2. Center the heading
3. Indent the paragraphs as shown
4. Underline as shown

```
WORD PROCESSING COMPUTER APPLICATIONS

Simply put, word processing is what it says:  the processing of
words.  Documents containing predominantly sttraight-copy copy
type use a word processing system and/or aplication for
processing.  Typically, documents such as letters, memos,
reports, manuscripts, and tabels come to mind.

Brief History:

    In th early 1960s IBM developed and markted the Masgnetic
Tape Selectric Typewriter (MTST).  This typeriter was the first
turely automated word procesing system with tape memory for
storage and errorr-free playback.  They were, of course, failry
expensive (aroudn $10,000 initially), and thus IBM also
introducded the concept of centralized word processing.  It
made much more sence to centrelize the system in a business so
that the machnine remained continually in use.  They were
ismpmly too expensive and too large to be a practical accessory
in every office
    Centralisation became the commonly thought of method of
perfroming word processing duties at this time.  Often the
bulky word processor was closeted away in the basement with the
unfortnate operater.  They also were not the quietest machines
around, but the technology was new and rather evolutionary.  At
that time it was an exciting piece of euqipment which gave
typists and office assistants a tool
by which to elimijnate the need for retyping numberous
drafts and applying their artistic talents to paper with
whiteout and erasers.  It also gave these oeperators a new kind
of status and a new title:  word processors.  They held a new
skills which was rapidly gorwing in demand.  Skilled
wordprocessors became the elite of office personnel and
qcquired a better salery as a result.
```

5. Save the document as HISTORY
6. Run a spelling check on the document
7. Change the left margin to 1.5 and the right margin to 5.5 using the following guidelines:

   in 4.2:
   a. Press **Shift F8**
   b. Choose **3**
   c. Type **the number for the left margin**
   d. Press **Enter**
   e. Type **the number for the right margin**
   f. Press **Enter**

   in 5.0:
   a. Press **Shift F8**
   b. Choose **L** for Line

c. Press **7** or **M** for Margins
d. Type **the left margin setting**
e. Press **Enter**
f. Type **the right margin setting**
g. Press **Enter**
h. Press **F7** to exit back to your document

8. Double space the entire document (HINT: **Shift F8** again)
9. Make the main heading bold
10. Create a header for the document and include the page number command (^N) in the header

```
Word Processing History/ 1960s through 1970s        Page ^P
```

11. Change the right margin to a ragged edge rather than justified:

<u>in 4.2:</u>
a. Move to the top of the document
b. Press **Ctrl F8**
c. Choose **3**
d. Press **Enter**

<u>in 5.0:</u>
a. Move to the top of the document
b. Press **Shift F8**
c. Choose **1** for Line
d. Choose **3**
e. Press **F7** to exit back to the document

12. Proof the document carefully and/or run a spelling check
13. Save the document as HISTORY
14. Print a copy of the report
15. Print a copy of only the second page of the report

NOTES

PRACTICE DOCUMENT 4: A REPORT WITH TABLE

Objectives:

The objectives of this exercise are to:

a. create various tab settings, including:
   a center tab
   a right-align tab
   a decimal tab
   a left-align tab
b. change tabs throughout a document more than one time
c. increase practice in setting up a multi-page document
d. view a document prior to printing

Type the document shown on Page 100 using the following guidelines:

1. Center the heading
2. Center the heading of the table
3. Change the right margin to 7.0
4. After typing the heading of the table, delete all tabs and set only the following tabs:

   a Center tab at 4.0 and 6.0

5. Type **the two column headings.** Press **Enter** twice after typing the column heading on the right.
6. Clear all tabs and set the following new tabs:
   a. a left (L) tab at .5
   b. a right-align tab (R) at 4.5
   c. a decimal tab (.) at 6.1
7. Type all lines through "Issaquah." Tab to .5 to begin the far left column
8. Stop on the line before TOTAL
9. Add a left-align tab at 1.5
10. Type the **"TOTAL"** line
11. Include the solid lines at the top and bottom of the table
12. Finish typing the document
13. Run a spelling check
14. Save the document as CENSUS
15. Print a copy of the report
16. Change the spacing in the report (except the table) to double
17. Create an appropriate header for the table. Include a page number in the header.
18. View the document to be sure it will print correctly
19. Save the document again
20. Print a copy of the revised document
21. Clear your screen

GROSS POPULATION

Of the eight areas that make up the East King Council service area (as defined for this project), by far the most populous is the Bellevue area, with 1/3 of the total population in 1980. The areas north and northeast of Bellevue (Kirkland, Redmond, Bear Creek, Bothell/Woodinville, and the Snohomish County Border tracts) together contain another 53-1/2 percent of the population, with Mercer Island and the growing East Sammamish/Issaquah area making up the remaining 13 percent.

Exhibit C displays the 1980 census figures for each of the eight areas and the proportion of the overall population residing in each.

EXHIBIT C: 1980 POPULATION

	1980 Population	Percentage of Total
Snohomish County Border tracts	29,600	9.5%
Bothell/Woodinville	71,471	23.3
Kirkland	22,851	7.4
Redmond	31,464	10.3
Bear Creek	8,909	2.9
Bellevue	101,828	33.2
Mercer Island	21,527	7.0
East Sammamish/ Issaquah	19,001	6.2%
TOTAL	306,597	

Anticipated growth by the year 2000* shows remarkable population increases to the north and east of Bellevue, from 90 percent growth in Bothell/Woodinville to 125 percent growth in East Sammamish/Issaquah. Growth expected in East Sammamish is most striking -- 176 percent.

* Source: Puget Sound Council of Governments

COMMAND SUMMARY

PREVIEW

This is a quick reference guide and should be used to look up functions only after completing all exercises in Section 2. Upon completion of the exercises, refer to this summary for quick reference to key functions.

Blocking Text

Use this command to assign special formats, move or copy text, and save blocks of text such as frequently used paragraphs.

1. Move to the beginning of the text to be blocked
2. Press **Alt F4**
3. Use arrow keys or other combination of keys to block the entire text
4. Perform editing or formatting commands
5. Pressing **Alt F4** again will turn block mode off

Centering Text

before typing:

1. **Shift F6**
2. Type **the text**
3. Press **Enter**
4. Press **Shift F6** again to turn off the Center command

after typing:

1. Block the text
2. Press **Shift F6**

Character Formatting

with 5.0 ONLY:

Use this feature to assign formats like italics and double underline as well as others.

1. Press **Ctrl F8**
2. Choose **2** or **A** for Appearance
3. Select style

NOTE: Character formatting with 4.2 is done through the Font command.

Copying Text

<u>in 4.2:</u>

1. Block the text
2. Press **Ctrl F4** (the Move command also used to copy)
3. Press **2** to Copy
4. Move to location to insert copy
5. Press **Ctrl F4** again
   and Choose **2** for paragraph

<u>with 5.0:</u>

1. Block Text
2. Press **Ctrl F4**
3. Choose **1** or **B**
4. Choose **2** or **C**
5. Move to location where you wish to copy text
6. Press **Enter**

Default Drive

<u>From a dual-disk or hard disk system</u>:

1. Press **F5**

A message appears in the lower right corner asking you to press the equals (=) sign to change the directory.

2. Press =

The A or C drive is shown.

3. Type **B:** (from a dual-disk system)

   or

   Type **A:** (from a hard disk system)

4. Press **Enter**

5. The new default directory prompt is now showing in the lower left corner of your screen

6. Press **Enter** again

You are now looking at the directory of the B Drive. Don't worry about your document. It is still in memory, and you can return to it quickly. You will learn more about this directory shortly. For now,

7. Press **F7** to return to your document

Displaying Print Jobs

Use this command to see all of the jobs you have sent to the printer.

<u>with 5.0:</u>

1. Press **Shift F7**
2. Choose **4** or **C**
3. Press **F7** to exit

FONTS AND POINTS

Change the size and style of your characters through the Font command.

<u>in 4.2:</u>

1. Press **Ctrl F8**
2. Choose **1**
3. Enter the **Pitch Number**
4. Press **Enter**
5. Enter the **Font Number**
6. Press **Enter**

<u>with 5.0:</u>

1. Press **Ctrl F8**
2. Choose **4** or **B** for Base font
3. Select font (point) style
4. Choose **1** or **S**

Hanging Indents

Use for itemized sentences or paragraphs, as well as instructions such those used in this guide.

1. Type the number at the left margin.
2. Use the F4 key rather than the Tab key to move to the 1.5 tab position (or any tab position at which you want the indent to occur)

3. Type the text, letting the right margin wrap
4. Continue this procedure for each itemized number

Headers and Footers

Create headers and/or footers for odd pages, even pages, or all pages.

<u>in 4.2:</u>

1. Move the cursor to the very top of the document
2. Press **Shift F8**
3. Choose **6**
4. Type **1** for the header number
5. Type the text heading
6. Press **F7** to exit

<u>with 5.0:</u>

1. Press **Shift F8**
2. Choose **2** or **P**
3. Choose **3** or **H**
4. Choose **1** for Header A
5. Choose the desired pages for the header to appear
6. Type the header
7. Choose **F7** to exit and save the new changes

Line Spacing

Move to the line in your text preceding the place at which you want to begin the spacing.

<u>in 4.2:</u>

These steps are displayed at the bottom of your screen and are fairly easy to follow.

1. Press **Shift F8**
2. Choose **4** to access the spacing options
3. Type **2** as the number of line spaces you want (for double spacing)
4. Press **Enter**

<u>in 5.0:</u>

1. Press **Shift F8**
2. Choose **1** or **L**
3. Choose **6** or **S**
4. Type the desired spacing (**2** or **3**)
5. Press **F7**

Moving Text

with 4.2:

1. Block the text
2. Choose **1** to move
3. Move the cursor to the location to which you want to move the block
4. Press **Ctrl F4** again
5. Choose **Option 5** (Text)

This combination is the Move command. The Copy and Move functions are located in the same function key command.

7. Choose **1** to cut block (in 4.2)

with 5.0:

1. Block the text to be moved
2. Press **Ctrl F4**
3. Choose **1** or **B**
4. Choose **1** or **M**
5. Move to new location in document
6. Press **Enter**

Printing Selected Pages

Method 1 with 4.2:

1. Position the cursor anywhere in Page 2 (or on the page in a long document which you want to print)
2. Press **Shift F7**
3. Choose **2** to send the page to the printer

The page on which your cursor is located will print.

or
Method 2:

1. Position the cursor on any page in a long document
2. Press **Shift F7**
3. Choose **4** for Printer Control
4. Choose **P** for Print a Document

You'll see a menu for typing the document name, so

5. Type the document name
6. Press **Enter**

To print selected pages:

7. Type the desired pages, such as **1-3** or **1-5, 6, 8**

in 5.0:

1. Press **Shift F7**
2. Choose **3** or **D**
3. Type document name
4. Press **Enter** for all pages or type the pages to be printed

Examples:

11, 17
11-17
10, 12-14

Printing Multiple Copies

in 4.2:

1. Press **Shift F7**
2. Choose **3** for print options
3. Choose **2** for number of copies
4. Type the number desired
5. Press **F7** to exit

in 5.0:

1. Press **Shift F7**
2. Choose **N**
3. Type the number of copies needed

Printing the Document

1. Press **Shift F7**
2. Choose **1** or **F**

Replacing Text

Use this command to search for and replace existing text.

1. Press **Alt F2**
2. Press **Y** to confirm replacement (if necessary)
3. Type word(s) for which you are searching
4. Press **F2**
5. Type the replacement text
6. Press **F2**
7. Confirm replacements and repeat

Restoring Deleted Text

Use the F1 key to see the previous two deletions.

1. Press **F1**
2. Choose **1** or **R** to Restore
3. Choose **2** or **P** to recall 2nd to the last deletion

Retrieving a Document

<u>from list files:</u>

1. Press **F5**
2. Press **Enter** to confirm directory
3. Select the file
4. Choose **1** to retrieve

<u>from F10:</u>

1. Press **Shift F10**
2. Type the name of the file
3. Press **Enter**

Reveal Codes

Use Reveal Codes to see all formats, tabs, indents, and other formatting codes. You may edit and delete formats in Reveal Codes as well as adding text.

1. Press **Alt F3** to turn Reveal Codes on and off.

Saving a Document

<u>from F7:</u>

1. Press **F7**
2. Press **Y** to Save
3. Press **Y** to Replace (if necessary)
4. Press **Y** or **N** to exit or to clear the screen

<u>from F10:</u>

1. Press **F10**
2. Type your document name or press **Enter** to the name showing
3. Press **Y** to Replace (if necessary)

Saving and Retrieving Blocks of Text

Use this feature to save frequently used blocks of text.

to save:

1. Block the text to be saved
2. Press **F10**
3. Give the block a name

to retrieve:

1. Press **F5**
2. Press **Enter** to the directory name
3. Select the filename you gave to the block of text
4. Choose **1** to Retrieve

Searching for Text

1. Press **F2**
2. Type text for which you are searching
3. Press **F2** to move to the first occurrence of this text
4. Keep pressing **F2** to move to remaining occurrences

Spelling

1. Press **Ctrl F2**
2. Choose **1** to enter path
3. Choose **3** or **D** to correct the document (or make another selection)

NOTE: If using a dual-disk system you should follow the screen messages for inserting the Spelling program into Drive B (if necessary).

Tab Settings

in 4.2:

1. Press **Shift F8**
2. Choose **1**
3. Press **Ctrl End** to delete all of the tab settings
4. Use your **Right Arrow** key to move to 2.5 on the ruler line.
5. Press **L** for a left-aligned tab setting at 2.5

<u>in 5.0:</u>

1. Press **Shift F8**
2. Choose **1**
3. Choose **8**
4. Set or clear tabs
5. Press **F7** to exit and save settings

Viewing the Document

Use the View option to see how your document is going to look when printed, prior to giving the print command.

1. Press **Shift F7**
2. Choose **6**
3. Choose **F7** to Exit View mode

NOTES

SECTION 3

SPREADSHEETS

PREVIEW

Spreadsheet programs like Lotus 1-2-3 and Joe Spreadsheet can be used to create trial balance sheets, payroll forms, income statements, business forecasts, and other financial reports.

Today, Lotus 1-2-3 is widely acknowledged as the best-selling electronic spreadsheet product of all time. Many users favor 1-2-3 for its easy-to-use command structure and great flexibility and power. If you are familiar with 1-2-3, it will take a very short time to become familiar with Joe Spreadsheet. Their menus are only slightly different. The primary difference between the two programs lies in the names of the commands found in the menus and submenus.

1-2-3 and Joe each combine three productivity functions—spreadsheets, presentation graphics, and data management—into a single package.

A spreadsheet is an electronic version of the large multi-columned paper accountants frequently use. When you use a spreadsheet program, you create a *worksheet* with your data organized into columns and rows. Your data can include words, numbers, and formulas. Each data item occupies a single *cell* at the intersection of a column and row. The monitor screen can show only a small section of the whole worksheet at a time. To bring different sections of a worksheet into view, you press the arrow keys on the keyboard. One of the most important features of a spreadsheet program is the *recalculation* feature that provides automatic recalculation of formulas on the worksheet when cell values are changed.

The *presentation graphics* feature allows users to quickly and easily graph spreadsheet data with bar charts, pie charts, and/or line charts. Normally, a chart is first prepared on the screen, and, if the image is satisfactory, it may be saved on disk and sent to the printer.

The *data management* feature provides users with a variety of file-handling functions (similar to those you will learn in the dBASE III PLUS section of this guide, and therefore discussed in more detail in that section). The most notable of these are extracting records having specific characteristics and sorting records on one or more fields. In 1-2-3 and Joe, each row of data is considered a record, while the worksheet columns are considered the record's fields.

The data management feature of 1-2-3 or Joe is not the primary or most powerful feature of these software programs. For that reason, this section of the guide will focus only on the spreadsheet features and postpone the database functions until Section 4.

USING THIS GUIDE

Instructions in this section are similar to those found earlier for WordPerfect. The steps used in the exercises are numbered. Any instructions that are slightly different in Joe than in 1-2-3 are detailed in parentheses next to the instruction. The instructional part of this section includes practice exercises that introduce various concepts and functions of 1-2-3 and Joe. Additional practice documents are found at the end of the section. These documents include some additional features, as well as providing practice using both 1-2-3 and Joe.

It is recommended, in order to best retain the material, that you proceed through this section in the order of presentation. You should also complete all exercises in this section.

BEGINNING SPREADSHEET FUNCTIONS

EXERCISE 3.1. HOW TO START 1-2-3 OR JOE

With a hard disk system:

1. Type **123** at the C> (or Type **JOE**)

2. Press **Enter**

With a dual-disk system:

1. Boot up your computer system with DOS in the usual way. When you have the A> on your screen, take the DOS out of Drive A, insert your 1-2-3 or Joe program into Drive A, and close the drive door (assuming "boot" is ok).

2. Type **123** (or Type **JOE**)

3. Press **Enter**

A fresh worksheet appears on your screen.

Figure 3 -1 illustrates the basic format of a 1-2-3 and a Joe worksheet. Both worksheets are constructed of rows and columns, which intersect to form cells. You can put words, numbers, or formulas into any of these cells. As you can see, there is very little difference between the worksheet formats. The primary differences are that (1) Joe inserts leading zeros on the row numbers that appear on the left side of the worksheet and (2) Joe shows the function key assignments on the third row of the control panel above the worksheet.

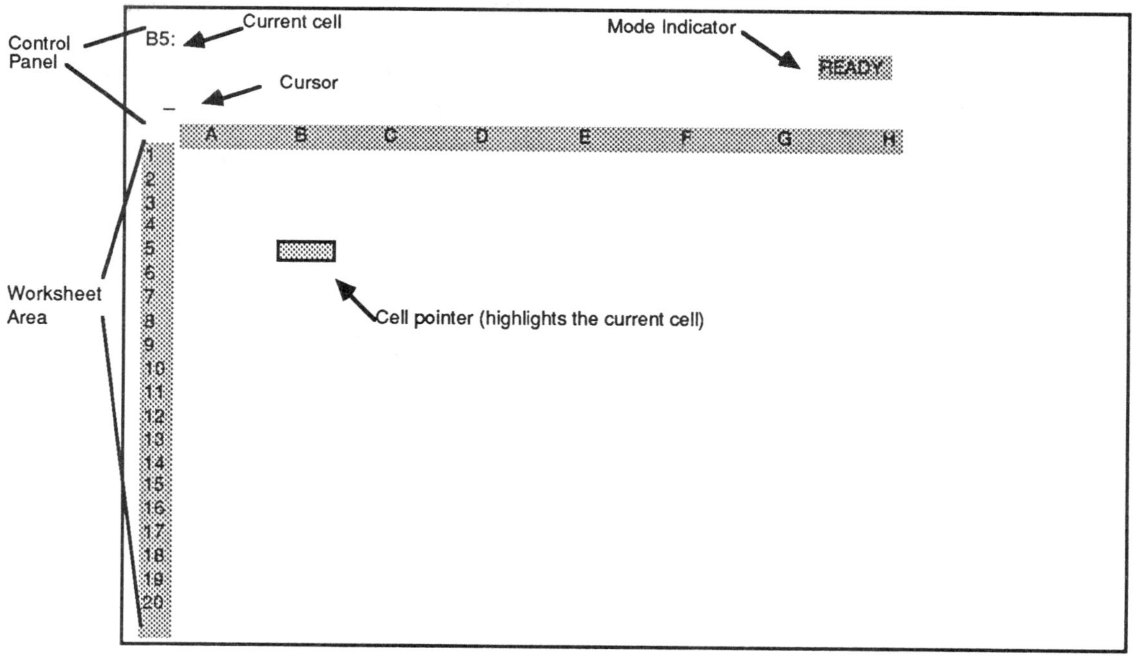

(a) 1-2-3

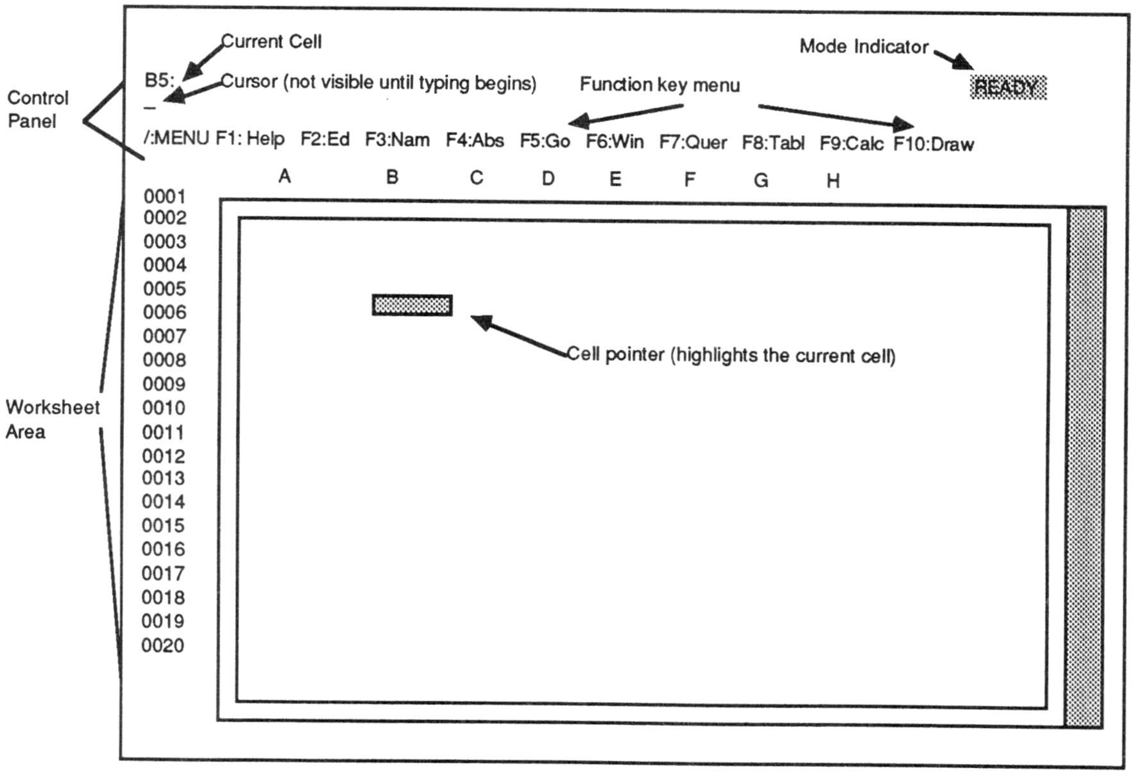

(b) Joe Spreadsheet

Figure 3-1. 1-2-3 and Joe Worksheets

Rows, Columns, and Cells

Look at your screen and at Figure 3-1. There are 20 *rows* (identified by numbers) and 8 nine-character-width *columns* (identified by letters now showing on the screen). The intersection of the rows and columns is referred to as a *cell*. Each cell is identified by its row and column coordinates. For example, Cell B5 is formed by Column B and Row 5. You can place either text (called labels) or numbers (called values) into any cell.

Worksheets can be very large. The screen you see represents only a small portion of the worksheet (a *window)* that, in fact, consists of either 2,048 or 8,192 rows and 256 columns. Repeated depression (holding down) of one of the four arrow keys will scroll other portions of the worksheet into the window.

To Move Through the Worksheet

Your highlight is now located in a cell on your worksheet. You can move from cell to cell by pressing the Up, Down, Left, and Right arrow keys. Other movements are shown in Figure 3-2.

1. Move your cursor around on the spreadsheet and then relocate it again in Cell A1 (or A0001 in Joe)

NOTE: Throughout these instructions, the cells will be referred to as A1, A2, B4, etc., even though in Joe they are shown on your screen as A0001, A0002, B0004, etc.

The movement keys, including the arrow keys are:

Up Arrow:	moves the pointer up one cell position
Down Arrow:	moves the pointer down one cell
Right Arrow:	moves the pointer right one cell
Left Arrow:	moves the pointer left one cell
PgUp:	moves the pointer up 20 lines (1 page)
PgDn:	moves the pointer down 20 lines (1 page)
Home:	moves the pointer to A1
End:	plus an arrow key, moves the pointer in the direction of the arrow in the last cell containing values or labels
Tab:	moves to the right one screen
Shift Tab:	moves to the left one screen
Scroll Lock:	when pressed, the worksheet moves with the cursor rather than remaining stationary as the cursor moves across it
F5:	used as the GoTo feature; pressing it allows you to enter a cell address to go to. For example, pressing **F5 A6** will cause the cursor to go to cell A6.

Figure 3-2. Cursor Movements

The Screen

Your screen consists of two primary areas:

- The control panel, which consists of the first three lines of the screen. It is here that you'll be developing words and numbers to put into the cells and also making selections from a command menu. The mode indicator shown in Figure 3-1 and located in the upper right corner of your screen is controlled entirely by the spreadsheet package. For example, a mode indicator of "READY" (showing now), means that the package is ready for you to type entries into a cell. A mode indicator of "WAIT," on the other hand, means that the package is occupied with a calculation and will not respond to any of your keystrokes. As you perform other functions, such as EDIT, the mode will change.

- The worksheet area, which shows a portion of the total number of rows and colums that compose the worksheet. After you enter data on the control panel, that data will also appear in the appropriate cell in the worksheet area, along with data previously entered into other cells.

The Current Cell

The *current cell* is the one that will receive the next data you enter. That cell is highlighted in the worksheet area on your screen with the *cell pointer*. The column and row coordinates of this cell are displayed in the upper left corner of the control panel. When you begin typing into a cell, the keystrokes appear in the upper left corner of the control panel. If you make a mistake, you can use the Backspace key to backtrack to the point of the error and retype the rest of the entry. If you want to bail out of this cell entirely, you can press the Escape key. Pressing the Enter key or an arrow key enters your typing into the cell pointer in the worksheet area. (After the arrow key is used, the cursor will be advanced one cell in the direction of the arrow.)

Types of Data

The data you enter on a worksheet will be either labels or values. Values can be used in calculations; labels cannot. There are three types of values: numeric values, formulas, and functions. Each cell can hold only one type of data, usually with a limited number of characters.

A *label* is used for descriptive spreadsheet entries and can consist of any combination of alphabetic, numeric, or special characters. A *numeric value* is simply a number. Sometimes you will fill a cell with a *formula* that directs the program to do a mathematical operation on numeric values in other cells. A cell can also contain a *function,* which is a predefined way to denote a commonly used formula. When you enter a formula or function into a cell on the control panel, the cell pointer on the worksheet area will show the numeric value resulting from the calculation. That value can in turn be used in other calculations. Also, the program will automatically recalculate the value of a formula or function if the value of related cells changes.

In 1-2-3 and Joe the first character of a cell entry tells the program what type of entry it is. Labels always start with a letter of the alphabet or the apostrophe character. Numeric values generally start with a digit, a decimal point, a dollar sign, or a plus or minus symbol. Formulas usually begin with a plus or minus symbol, decimal point, or a left parenthesis. Functions always begin with the @ sign. It is very important to get the first character of an entry correct so that the program is able to read the data and do the desired calculations.

Examples of labels and values are shown in Figure 3-3.

Example	Description	Entered on the Keyboard As
Revenue	Label	Revenue
Expenses	Label	Expenses
.15	Numeric Value	.15
$2,000,000	Numeric Value	$2,000,000
.6*A5/100-B2	Formula	.6*A5/100-B2
SUM(A1..A4)	Function	@SUM(A1..A4)
C3-D2	Formula	+C3-D2
3rd Quarter	Label	'3rd Quarter (with apostrophe added)

Figure 3-3. Examples of Different Types of Data

To Quit 1-2-3 or Joe

To leave the worksheet at the end of any session, you must access the command menus. These menus will be covered in more detail as you progress through this section, but, for now, practice exiting the program as instructed below. You may then quit until the next session or continue by restarting the program as directed at the beginning of this exercise.

1. To access the command menus press /

2. To Quit press **Q**

You will return to the system prompt.

Review Questions on Exercise 3.1

1. A spreadsheet program can be compared to an ____________________ worksheet.

2. A worksheet in a spreadsheet program consists of ______ and ________ that create a sort of grid on the screen.

3. The intersection of the rows and columns in a worksheet is called a ________.

4. To load the spreadsheet program, what should you type at the system prompt?

5. The control panel consists of which lines in your worksheet screen?

6. The mode indicator is located where on your screen?

7. How many keys are available for cursor movement functions in the spreadsheet program?

8. A spreadsheet program uses a label and a value in different ways. How are they used?

9. What symbol is used to begin writing a function?

10. What symbol is used to begin writing a formula?

11. What keystrokes are used to quit a session with 1-2-3 or Joe?

Answers to the Review Questions on Exercise 3.1

1. accounting 2. rows and columns
3. cell 4. 123 or Joe 5. the top three lines
6. the upper right corner 7. approximately 11
8. a label is not used for calculations; values are
9. @ 10. + 11. / Q (for Quit)

EXERCISE 3.2. HOW TO USE SPREADSHEET COMMANDS

1. Sign on to 1-2-3 or Joe as shown in Exercise 3.1

When the command menu is summoned by pressing the slash (/) key, the highlight on Line 2 of the control panel is positioned on the command that can be selected by pressing the Enter key or the first character of the command word. Options available by pressing Enter with the highlighted choice appear on Line 3. Figure 3-4 describes the ten main commands in 1-2-3 and Joe. Note that corresponding commands each begin with the same letter.

SPREADHSEET COMMANDS

1-2-3 Command	Joe Command	Explanation
Worksheet	WorkSets	This command allows you to do things that affect the entire worksheet. For example, it allows you to change the width of one or more columns, or to insert or delete columns or rows.
Range	RangeOps	This command allows you to perform operations on a portion of the worksheet.
Copy	CopyRan	This command allows you to copy any portion of the worksheet into another place on the worksheet.

(Continued)

(Continued)

SPREADHSEET COMMANDS

1-2-3 Command	Joe Command	Explanation
Move	MoveRan	This command lets you relocate any portion of the worksheet into another place on the worksheet.
File	File	This command enables you to access your disk to save, retrieve, or combine worksheets.
Print	Print	This command allows you to print any portion of your worksheet.
Graph	Graph	This command enables you to create graphs from your worksheet. The computer system must be equipped with a graphics display board for this command to be used effectively.
Data	Database	This command enables you to use the data management routines, to sort data, group data, or retrieve records with specific characteristics.
System	System	This command lets you temporarily leave your spreadsheet package in order to issue DOS commands.
Quit	Quit	This command ends your 1-2-3 or Joe session and enables you to return to DOS.

Figure 3-4. Command Set in 1-2-3 and Joe

To Set the Default

One of the first things you should do each time you sign on to the spreadsheet program is set your default drive to indicate the drive that holds your formatted data diskette (for saving files). You probably remember setting the default when using WordPerfect. Now you must go through the process when working with 1-2-3 or Joe. This is an essential step so that all of your worksheets are automatically saved on your data diskette and not with your program files in A or C. If you have a hard-disk system, your data diskette will be in Drive A. If you have a dual-disk system, your data diskette will probably be in Drive B.

To set the default, do the following:

In 1-2-3:

1. Type **/FD** for File Directory

2. Type **A:** (hard disk) or **B:** (dual-disk)

3. Press **Enter**

In Joe:

1. Type **/WGDD Esc** for WorkSets Global Default Directory Esc

2. Type **A:** (hard disk) or **B:** (dual-disk)

3. Press **Enter**

4. Press **U** to Update the setting

5. Press **Q** to Quit and return to the READY mode

To Enter Labels

You are now ready to type in data for the sales table worksheet shown below:

	A	B	C	D
1	AGENT	Region A	Region B	Totals
2	Michaels	500	200	700
3	Adams	200	100	300
4	Williams	50	400	450
5	Jones	100	700	800
6	Totals	850	1400	2250

The procedure will be to move to the appropriate cell using the arrow keys; type a value or label; press Enter or the arrow keys to move to another cell.

1. Move to Cell A1 using the arrow keys (you may already be there)

2. Type **AGENT**

NOTE: It will automatically be recognized as a label because it begins with a character.

3. Press **Enter**

NOTE: If you make an error as you are keying values or labels into cells, use the Backspace key to backtrack to the point of the error and retype the remainder of the entry. You can watch this process in the control panel.

After you press Enter, you will notice that AGENT, a label, has been transferred to the very top line of the control panel and is shown as: 'AGENT. The apostrophe is there to inform you that this entry is being stored as a label. You will also notice that "AGENT" has been sent to Cell A1 in the worksheet area.

3. Move to Cell B1 by pressing the **Right Arrow** key

4. Type **Region A**

5. Press **Enter** (or you may just move to another cell with the arrow keys)

Repeat Steps 3 through 5 for cells C1 and D1, entering the appropriate titles, then

6. Move to Cell A2 by pressing the arrow keys

7. Type **Michaels**

8. Move to Cell A3 by pressing the **Down Arrow** key

9. Type **Adams**

Continue entering the names through Cell A6.

To Enter Numeric Values

When you have finished entering all of the labels, you are ready to enter the numeric values. You will enter values in Cells B2 through C5 only. Do not enter values for B6, C6, and D6. You will enter formulas (later in this exercise) so that all of the total amounts will be calculated automatically.

NOTE: B2 through C5 includes all cells between these two going both down and across. They are B2 through B5 and C2 through C5. Note this portion of the worksheet area on your screen. It is considered a *range* in both 1-2-3 and Joe (ranges are discussed in more detail later).

1. Move to Cell B2

2. Type **500**

3. Move to Cell C2 by pressing the arrow keys

4. Type **200**

5. Move to Cell B3

6. Type **200**

Continue this procedure for Cells C3 through C5 and Cells B4 through B5.

To Enter Formulas

You are now ready to enter formulas that will automatically compute the totals and enter the results in the worksheet cells.

1. Move to Cell D2

2. Type **+B2+C2**

This formula will compute the total for Cells B2 and C2, which compose all of Michaels's figures.

3. Press the **Down Arrow** once to move to Cell D3

When you move, the correct sum is placed in Cell D2 on the worksheet.

4. Type the correct formula for computing Adams's total: **+B3+C3**

5. Move with the arrow keys to D4

Enter the following formulas for the remainder of your total cells.

Cell D4: **+B4+C4**
Cell D5: **+B5+C5**
Cell B6: **+B2+B3+B4+B5**
Cell C6: **+C2+C3+C4+C5**
Cell D6: **+B6+C6**
or
Cell D6: **+D2+D3+D4+D5**

You are entering the formula for D6 last since the value of this cell can only be established after formulas are set up for calculating the other totals.

Operators

An *operator* is a character used in a formula that tells the program to perform a certain calculation.

There are other operators you can use in addition to the plus sign (+). They are:

^ exponentiation
* multiplication
/ division
- subtraction

The hierarchy, or order of precedence, is as follows:

a. exponentiation is performed first
b. multiplication and division are performed next, in the order in which they occur
c. addition and subtraction are last, in the order in which they occur

The following formula shows you an example of the hierarchy:

+B8/D23+A2*F3^2

This formula results in the following hierarchy:

a. the value of F3 is raised to the power of 2
b. the value in B8 is divided by the value in D23
c. the value in A2 is multiplied by the result of Step a
d. the result of Step b is added to the result of Step c

When parentheses are used to surround parts of the formula, the operation inside the parentheses is given precedence over any other part of the formula.
As in the example below:

+D2-(C23+D23)

C23 and D23 are first added together. The result is then subtracted from the value in D2.

To Save the Worksheet

You can save or retrieve files on disk by again invoking menus. For example, to save the worksheet on which you are currently working, do the following:

In both 1-2-3 and Joe:

1. To get the command menu, press /

2. Press **F** for File

3. Press **S** for Save

You now have a message on the screen asking for the name under which you want to save this worksheet (file).

4. Type the name **DOC1**

5. Press **Enter**

The worksheet is now saved as B:DOC1.WKS on a dual-disk system (or as A:DOC1.WKS if using a hard disk system) in 1-2-3. The filename would be B:DOC1.WKQ (or A:) if using Joe.

With any of your documents, the file extensions will remain the same as those stated here. If using 1-2-3, it will always be the .WKS extension and with Joe it will always be the .WKQ extension. These extensions are inserted automatically. You do not need to type them.

Filenames may be up to eight characters in length and must not include spaces. They may include the underscore mark (_) between characters. Always begin the filename with a character, although at other locations in the name you may include both numeric and alphabetic characters.

6. To quit the program, type **/Q**

Review Questions on Exercise 3.2

1. The command set (menus) are accessed by pressing which key?

2. List several of the options available through the first main set of commands.

3. List the steps used with your program to set the default drive.

4. List the hierarchy of operators used with 1-2-3 or Joe.

5. List the steps used to save a worksheet.

Answers to the Review Questions on Exercise 3.2

1. Slash key (/) 2. See Figure 3-4

3. In 1-2-3:
   - a. Type **/FD** for File Directory
   - b. Type **A:** (hard disk) or **B:** (dual-disk)
   - c. Press **Enter**

   In Joe:
   - a. Type **/WGDD Esc** for WorkSets Global Default Directory Esc
   - b. Type **A:** (hard disk) or **B:** (dual-disk)
   - c. Press **Enter**
   - d. Press **U** to Update the setting
   - e. Press **Q** to Quit and return to the READY mode

4. ^ exponentiation
   / * division and multiplication, in the order in which they appear
   + - addition and subtraction, in the order in which they appear

5. /FS

EXERCISE 3.3. HOW TO EDIT A WORKSHEET

1. To start the program, type **123** (or type **JOE**)

At some point, you may want to change the values and labels entered in cells. Perhaps a word was misspelled in a label, a value was entered incorrectly, or you wish to observe the effect of a change on the worksheet. There are three basic ways in which you can change the contents of a cell. You can:

- a. simply move to the cell to be changed and retype the contents
- b. erase the contents through the command set
- c. use the EDIT mode (F2 key) to insert or delete characters or numbers

First, you need to retrieve your worksheet.

To Retrieve a Worksheet

You have saved your worksheet. Once the worksheet is saved, you can retrieve it from the data disk drive (either A or B). Each time you sign on at the beginning of the day, you will want to either begin a new spreadsheet or retrieve a stored worksheet from the data disk. You can also retrieve stored files when a worksheet is in the window. The retrieved file will replace the one in the window. As long as the worksheet in the window was saved, you do not need to worry about losing it.

1. Type **/FR** for File Retrieve (in 1-2-3) or **R** for Reload (in Joe)

The prompt asking for the name of the file to retrieve appears.

2. Move the arrow keys so that "DOC1" is highlighted (it may already be on DOC1)

3. Press **Enter**

As with saving, the .WKS or .WKQ extension and the drive are assumed as long as the default drive is set. You could also have typed the document name rather than highlighting it.

To Edit with the F2 Key

1. Move to Cell B4 by pressing the arrow keys

2. Press **F2**

At this time you can use the arrow keys and the Del key to make changes in the value now showing in the upper left corner of your screen.

3. Press the **Left Arrow** key to move the cursor to the 5 in 50

4. Type **1** (watch the screen as you do so; the 50 moves to the right)

5. Press **Enter** when the number is reading 150

NOTE: Not only did your value of 50 change to 150 but all totals affected by that number changed automatically as well. More is discussed on this later.

6. Press **F2** again with the cursor still in B4

7. Move your cursor to the 1 in 150

8. Press the **Del** key and **Enter**

9. Move to Cell A3

10. Press **F2**

11. To change the name to "Adamson," move the cursor to the space next to s and type **on**

12. Press **Enter**

NOTE: Any value or label may be edited using the F2 key. This is particularly valuable when you have created long formulas and do not want to key them in from the start.

To Erase Cell Contents from the Command Set

You can also make changes through the command set by erasing the contents of a cell and then either leaving the cell blank or adding new contents to it.

To erase the contents:

1. Move to Cell A1

2. Type **/RE** for Range (1-2-3) or RangeOps (Joe) Erase

3. Press **Enter**

The cell contents are gone.

4. Type **AGENTS** again in Cell A1

EXERCISE 3.4. HOW TO USE THE RECALCULATION FEATURE

Now it's time to do some experimenting, to explore the power that spreadsheets give to you. The automatic *recalculation* feature in spreadsheets means that if a cell value being changed contains a function or formula that affects the amounts in other cells in the worksheet, the other cells will be adjusted automatically. Let's experiment with the recalculation feature:

1. Move to Cell B2

2. Change Michaels's Region A sales from **500** to **600**

NOTE: Not only did the value in Cell B2 change, but it also changed in Cell B6 from 850 to 950, in Cell D2 from 700 to 800, and in Cell D6 from 2250 to 2350. Every cell whose value depended on the value in Cell B2 also changed.

The recalculation feature makes electronic spreadsheets a

valuable tool. Most businesses go through an extensive series of "what if" scenarios when making key decisions. For example:

> What if Region A totals are 10 percent lower next month?
>
> What if Williams increases Region A sales to 500?

There is a need to constantly recalculate dozens of interdependent figures on schedules to find out the ultimate effect if something happens. Computations that spreadsheets can do in seconds could take hours to do by hand. Practice with your worksheet. Try the following exercises, watching closely as the changes take place:

3. Change Adams's Region B sales from **100** to **500**
4. Change Williams's Region A sales from **50** to **-50**
5. Try some others on your own
6. Change the worksheet back to its original format

More on the Command Set

You have used the command set for functions such as to save and retrieve files as well as to quit the program and set the default drive. There is much more you can do with the command set. In fact, most of the features available to you in either 1-2-3 or Joe are found through this set of commands.

To Change the Column Width

You will want to change the width of your column anytime the values or labels are wider than the default width of nine characters. In this exercise you will change the width to accommodate wide labels.

With your highlight in any cell in Column A,

1. Press **Slash** (/)

As you know, commands may be selected in one of two ways:

a. Using the arrow keys to move the highlight to the desired choice and then pressing the Enter key
b. Typing the first letter of the menu or submenu (e.g., W, R, C, or Q)

2. Press the **Right Arrow** key and watch the screen as your highlight moves across the command selections

NOTE: As you do so, the third line of the panel changes as well. This line is showing you the subcommand options available under whatever main command option you have highlighted.

In this way you can preview the choices available without leaving the main command options.

3. Press **W** for Worksheet (1-2-3) or WorkSets (Joe)

A new list of options appears.

4. Press **C** for Column (1-2-3) or Columns (Joe)

This option allows you to change the width of your column. Your highlight is presently in Column A, so this is the one you will change.

Once again, a new list of commands appears. Remember, you are continuing to move down into submenus of your original choice, Worksheet or WorkSets.

You can see that you have a few choices open to you. You want to change the width of the column containing your highlight on the worksheet.

5. Press **S** to Set-Width (1-2-3) or Set_column_width (Joe)

You must now set the width. The message tells you that you can set widths in the range of either 1 through 72 (1-2-3) or 1 through 240 (Joe). For this column, your longest name will not be more than 20 characters.

6. Type **20**

7. Press **Enter**

The menus now disappear, and you have returned to your worksheet in the Ready mode.

You can see that the first column (Column A) is now much wider than the other columns.

In abbreviated form, what you have just done is:

In 1-2-3:

/ Worksheet **C**olumn **S**et **20 Enter**

In Joe:

/ WorkSets **C**olumns **S**et_column_width **20 Enter**

Although there are some differences when using Joe and 1-2-3, the commands usually begin with the same letter. This is perhaps another justification for using the letter to reach commands and subcommands when making selections.

Throughout the remainder of this section, instructions will be given using the abbreviated format shown here.

With your first column wider,

8. Change each name in Column A by moving to the cell and then retyping the names as follows. Remember, retyping values or labels when the cursor is located in the cell replaces the cell contents.

   Ted Michaels
   Elise Adamson
   Sam Williams
   Terry Jones

To Escape

As mentioned earlier in this section, any time you are moving through the menus, and you decide you want to back out of a menu, simply use the *Esc* key. Pressing it once will put you back to the previous command options; pressing it twice will put you back two options, and so on. You can escape right back to the READY mode in your worksheet and start over if you so choose.

If you have been making selections in the command sequence (from each list of commands and subcommands), you can still back out with the Escape key. The commands do not go into effect until you have performed the last step in the sequence, from the very last submenu, and pressed Enter.

9. Save your worksheet again.

   Type **/FS** and press **Enter**

   At the message asking whether you want to replace the file, press **R** for Replace. This message will appear each time you are saving a file that has already been saved once.

10. Quit for this session. Complete the following review questions.

Review Questions on Exercises 3.3 and 3.4

1. What are the three methods of changing the contents of a cell?

2. List the steps required to retrieve a worksheet.

3. What happens when a value is changed in a cell containing a formula or function?

4. List the steps necessary to change the width of a column.

5. If you are into your third set of subcommands and realize that you do not want to save the changes you have been making and would like to return to the READY mode, what can you do?

6. What message appears when saving a file that has already been saved to the data disk at least one time?

Answers to the Review Questions on Exercises 3.3 and 3.4

1. (a) /RE (to erase the contents of a cell or range of cells)
(b) F2 Edit key (c) type a new entry and press **Enter**
2. /FR, type or choose the name of the file, press **Enter**
3. All other cells containing values that are affected by the formula or function will have their values automatically adjusted
4. /WCS , type the new width, **Enter**
5. Press **Esc** 6. A message asking whether you want to replace the old file

EXERCISE 3.5. HOW TO PRINT A WORKSHEET

For Joe Users ONLY

Installing a printer with Joe:

First, sign on to Joe.

If you have not installed the printer you will be using with Joe, follow the installment steps listed below. If worksheets have been printed with your disk before, you can skip the installment instructions.

1. Type the following sequence of menu commands:

   /WGDIP for WorkSets Globals Defaults Install Printer

A list of printers supported by Joe will then be displayed. Select the correct printer from the list. Your choice will be recorded in a configuration file stored with your copy of Joe, and Joe will default to that choice the next time you use it. Therefore, this is the only time you will need to install the printer unless you start using a different kind of printer.

2. Press **Enter** when finished

3. To quit this menu, press **Q**

For Both 1-2-3 and Joe Users

1. Retrieve the worksheet called DOC1

then

2. As the series of menus appear, type **/PPR** for Print Printer (1-2-3) or Printer_Output (Joe) Range (1-2-3) or Range_to_print (Joe)

You must now enter the range of cells to print. The range includes the entire block on your worksheet that contains all of the cells you want to print. It is the area from the upper left corner to the lower right corner. This is usually Cell A1 through another cell on the lower right corner. The range of cells must always be entered before printing.

3. Type **A1..E3** as the range of cells in your present worksheet

4. Press **Enter**

Next, you are ready to give the go-ahead instruction. The range is set, and you are ready to print the worksheet. Be sure your printer is on and that you are on line to it.

5. Press **G** for Go

To leave the command mode, you choose the Quit option from the same submenu.

6. Press **Q** for Quit

NOTE: You could press G for Go several times without resetting the range to get multiple copies of your worksheet.

7. You can quit the program by typing **/Q**

INTERMEDIATE SPREADSHEET FUNCTIONS

PREVIEW

There are many other spreadsheet operations that will be useful, in addition to the commands you have learned. Among these operations are showing dollar amounts, using functions, moving rapidly around the worksheet, inserting or deleting rows or columns, moving cell contents, copying cell contents, creating separator lines, and using the presentation graphics feature.

EXERCISE 3.6. HOW TO FORMAT A WORKSHEET

There are two kinds of formats—global and range—which will both be discussed in this exercise. Formatting means that you are going to apply special features to the values on your worksheet. As you have been typing the values, you have been entering simple figures and whole numbers. Now it is time to make the numbers take on characteristics that give more information about what they are showing you. For example, you may wish to show some or all values as dollar amounts or percentages.

To Assign Global Format

Assigning a global format means that on the entire worksheet all will be shown in the same way. There are many global format options available to you.

1. Sign on to the program and create a new worksheet using the information shown in Figure 3-5 on the following page

NOTE: When you start 1-2-3 or Joe, you're automatically in a new worksheet file. If you are continuing from your previous exercise, you'll need to erase your screen from the last exercise with the following command sequence:

Type **/WEY** and press **Enter**

2. Set the default drive if you are just signing on

IMPORTANT NOTE: When you enter the information on Figure 3-5, type the main heading in B1 and let it overlap into Cell C1. When there are no values or labels in the cells to the right of a long entry, it will appear in the blank space. When there are values or labels in the cells to the right, however, the worksheet cell will show only the number of characters that use up the width of the cell, and the cell width must be adjusted.

You will also need to adjust the width of the columns to accommodate the widest label or value in the column. You may do this before or after entering the labels. If you wait until after, however, the labels will overlap each other until you adjust the width. (Hint: /WCS)

	A	B	C	D	E
1		SOFTWARE·PRODUCT·SALES			
2					..%
3	Product	..Last·Month	This·Month	Difference	Change
4					
5					
6	Word·				
7	Processing				
8	Software:	5013.98	5589.18		
9					
10	Database				
11	Software:	4918.72	5890.20		
12					
13	Spreadsheet				
14	Software:	3981.90	3544.32		
15					
16	Graphics				
17	Software:	9873.20	9672.20		
18					
19	Other:	6988.10	5233.38		

Figure 3-5. DOC2 Worksheet

To save the worksheet as DOC2, use the following command sequence:

3. Type **/FS** for File Save

4. Type the name **DOC2**

5. Press **Enter**

To be able to assign a global format, you'll need to move through a series of menus. On each menu, you'll type one letter to indicate your choice.

6. Type **/W** for Worksheet (or WorkSets in Joe)

7. Press **G** for Global (or Globals in Joe)

8. Press **F** for Format

From this format submenu you can make several selections. In this exercise you will be choosing the currency format for the values on your worksheet meaning that all values will appear with dollar signs, commas, and decimal digits.

The format submenu appears when giving either a global or a range command. You just gave a global command, because you want all values on the worksheet to be in currency format. You may at times, however, want only some of the numbers to be formatted (a range or group of cells, such as a column). When that is the case, you would type the following sequence to indicate menu choices:

/WRF for Worksheet Range Format

in either 1-2-3 or Joe. Using either the Global or Range command, you will have the following format options:

<u>Scientific</u>. Displays values in the exponential scientific format. The exponent is expressed as a power of 10 and is shown as an "E", such as 1:45E.

<u>General</u>. The default numeric displays and suppresses zeroes after the decimal point

<u>Percent</u>. Displays the values followed by a percent sign. The number of decimal places may also be set.

<u>Date</u>. You can specify the date format using this option.

The date choices are:

DD-MMM-YY (Example: 05-Nov-91)
DD-MMM (Example: 05-Nov)
MMM-YY (Nov-91)
(Long Intn'l) (05/05/91)
(Short Intn'l) (05/05)

<u>Text</u>. Displays the formula used in a cell rather than the result of the formula

<u>Hidden</u>. Will hide the contents of the cell so that it is not displayed on the screen or in print. This option is useful if you want to make comments that you want to read in the command line but do not want to see on the worksheet.

<u>Reset</u>. Will change a format from a range setting back to a global setting

9. To choose the currency option on the Format menu, type **C**

10. Press **Enter** to accept the default of 2 places to the right of the decimal

The commands you just invoked did the following:

Global(s). Tells the program you want to take an action that will affect the entire worksheet

Format. Enables you to format entries in a certain way

Currency. Tells the spreadsheet that you want dollar signs, commas (in appropriate places), and decimal digits in values

2. Sets the number of places to the right of the decimal place (you did not neet to type "2" because this is the default setting)

In this worksheet, your cells were changed so they were wide enough to accommodate the widest number after the dollar signs and decimal points were added. Sometimes, you adjust the width of the number in a cell by editing it and making the number too large for a cell. When that happens, a row of asterisks (****************) will appear in the cell where the formatted number should be. The asterisks will disappear as soon as you widen the width of the column and the value will replace them.

11. Remember to save your worksheet (again) as DOC2.

To Use Functions

Both 1-2-3 and Joe have a number of useful functions that can save you a great deal of time in entering formulas. A *function* is a prestored formula. All functions in 1-2-3 and Joe are identified by some keyword (such as SUM, AVG, or IF) and preceded by the @ character. Two of the easiest functions to learn are SUM and AVG.

When you use either the SUM or AVG functions, you may need to identify the *range* of cells to be used to calculate your sum or average. You identified a range of cells when printing a copy of your worksheet. In that exercise, the range was from the upper left corner to the lower right corner of your worksheet, thus taking in the entire worksheet. The range concept is also useful if you want to move, copy, insert, delete, sort, and graph values shown on the worksheet. A range can include any group of cells, even those appearing in the middle of the worksheet. For example, D10..F14 is also a valid range of cells.

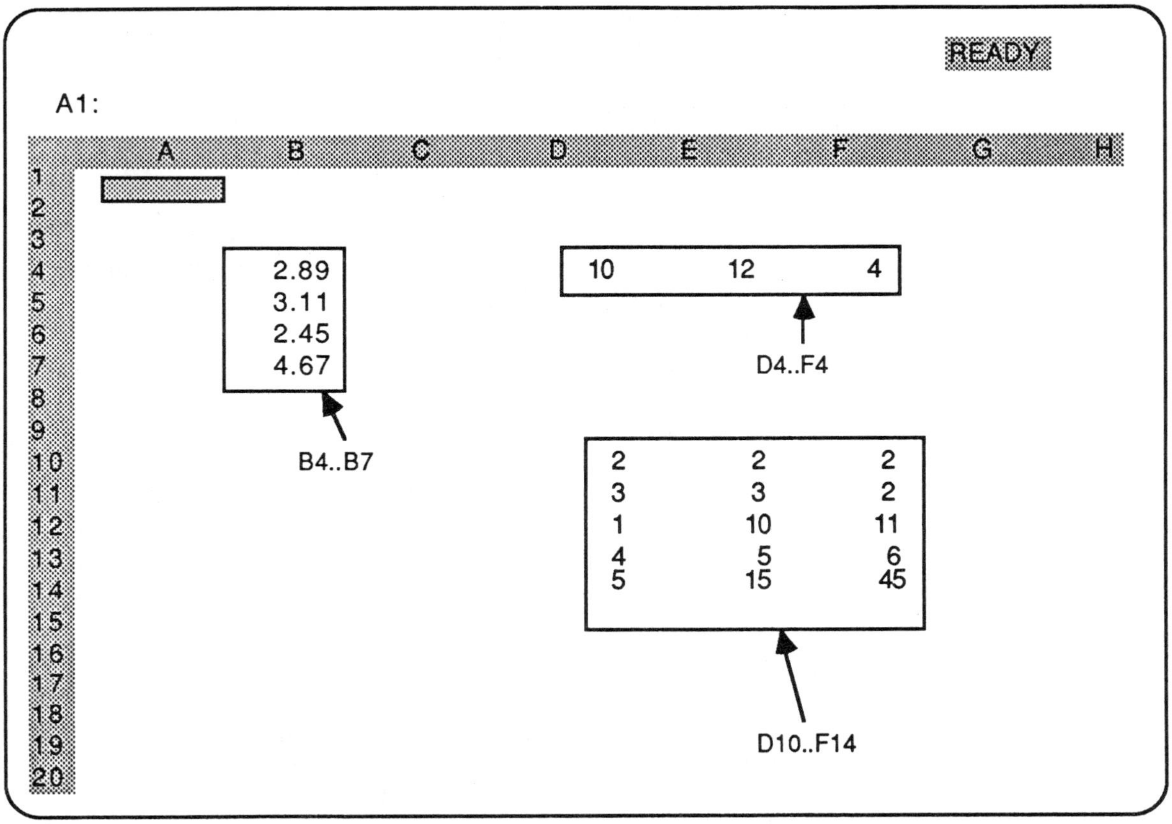

Figure 3-6. Examples of a Range of Cells

Look at Figure 3-6. The cell your cursor is located in at the time you enter the function and cell range is the cell that will contain the answer when the formula is performed.

Remember, the correct form for identifying a range of cells is to separate the starting and ending cell name by two periods. For example, if your cursor is in Cell A1 and you type the formula,

@SUM(B4..B11),

you are adding the values in Cells B4 through B11. The answer will be placed in Cell A1.

You can, of course, position your highlight in any cell on the worksheet and write a formula that performs a calculation involving cells in any other location on the worksheet.

The @SUM Function

Use the @SUM function to add together a range of values in your DOC2 worksheet.

1. Move to Cell A21

2. Type the following label:

   Total

3. Move to Cell B21

4. Type the following formula. Watch the command line as you are typing the formula:

   @SUM(B8..B19)

5. Press **Enter**

The sum appears in Cell B21. This method, as you can see, is much faster than typing +B8+B11+B14+B17, etc. This is particularly true as the range of cells becomes longer.

The @AVG Function

The @AVG function works similarly to the @SUM. For example, @AVG (B8..B19) will calculate the average of values in a range of cells, B8 through B19. The function @AVG will sum the values in B8 through B19 and then divide the number of values into the sum to get the average.

1. Type the following title into Cells A23 and A24

   Monthly
   Average:

2. Move to Cell B24

3. Type the following AVG formula:

   @AVG(B8..B19)

4. Press **Enter**

The average appears in Cell B24.

5. Save the worksheet, replacing the original copy of DOC2

Other Spreadsheet Functions

More functions are shown in Figure 3-7. Further explanation of these as well as a more extensive list of available functions is available in a 1-2-3 or Joe reference manual.

Arithmetic and Statistical Functions: @SUM (range) calculates the sum of all values in a range @MAX (range) finds the highest value in a range @MIN (range) finds the lowest value in a range @COUNT (range) counts the number of nonempty cells in a range @STD (range) calculates the standard deviation of values	@PMT (present value, rate, number of payments) calculates an annuity (period payment) that is equivalent to a given present value at a specified interest rate @NPV (rate, range) calculates the present value of the cash flows in a range, at a specified interest rate
Other Functions: @ABS calculates the absolute value @LN calculates the natural logarithm of an argument @LOG calculates the base 10 logarithm of the argument @SQRT calculates the square root of the argument	Conditional Functions: @IF (conditional expression, value if true, value if false) supplies a cell with a value that depends on whether the conditional expression is true or false @CHOOSE (pointer value, list of possible values) chooses one value in a list of values, based on the pointer value
Financial Functions: @ PV (period payment, rate, number of payments) calculates the present value of an annuity, at a specified interest rate @FV (period payment, rate, number of payments) calculates the future value of an annuity, at a specified interest rate	Date Functions: @TODAY calculates today's date in 1-2-3 (in days since December 31, 1899*). Called @NOW in Joe. @DATE (year, month, day) calculates the number of days that have elapsed since the date specified in the argument and December 31, 1899*

*December 31, 1899, serves as a fixed reference point. In combination, the TODAY (NOW) and DATE functions can be used to calculate such things as the number of days past due on invoices or the number of days that an account has been in existence. In order for the value of a date function to look familiar (e.g., 12/15/90), you must appropriately format the cell in which the value appears.

Figure 3-7. Function Chart

6. Quit and continue to the review questions, or complete the review questions and continue

Review Questions on Exercise 3.6

1. Name the two types of formatting commands and describe each one.

2. How do you set a format that will affect the entire worksheet?

3. How do you set a format that will affect only certain cells on the worksheet?

4. If the following function, @AVG(C12..C20), is typed into Cell C25, what will be the result?

5. How would you write a function using the @ sign that would sum all values in Cells D2 through G2?

Answers to the Review Questions on Exercise 3.6

1. global and range. The global format affects the entire worksheet; range affects only specific cells on the worksheet.
2. /WGF 3. /RF 4. The values in C12 through C20 are summed and then the total is divided by the total number of cells in this range, and the result is put into Cell C25.
5. @SUM(D2..G2)

EXERCISE 3.7. HOW TO COMPLETE YOUR WORKSHEET

1. Sign onto 1-2-3 or Joe and retrieve DOC2

In this exercise, you will give your worksheet its finishing touches. There are many other options available to you through the command set. When finished, your worksheet will take on a polished appearance and will function as a useful worksheet tool.

To Use a Relative Address When Copying a Formula

One of the most convenient and most used copy commands is relative replication or relative addressing. This concept means that when you copy a formula from its location in one cell to another cell, the cell addresses within the formula change automatically to adjust to the addresses within the row and column to which you have moved.

Watch what happens when you copy the formulas you have created on the DOC2 worksheet.

In both 1-2-3 and Joe:

1. Move to Cell B21

NOTE: The sum of the cells in the formula appears in this cell in the worksheet area, but the command line shows the formula used to arrive at this value.

2. Type /C for Copy (1-2-3) or CopyRan (Joe)

When the message appears asking for the range to copy from, you can simply press Enter, since your highlight is already in the cell from which you want to copy.

3. Press **Enter**

4. At the message, asking for the range to copy to, type:

    C21

5. Press **Enter**

The formula has been copied to C21, and the resulting value is inserted there in the worksheet area.

6. Move to Cell C21 and look at the formula

NOTE: The cell ranges in the formula have automatically changed to C8..C19 from the original B8..B19. This is an example of relative addressing.

7. Copy the formula in B24 to C24 using the same procedure

To Use an Absolute Address

Absolute addressing allows you to designate certain cells as those that will not change when copied.

1. Move to Cell F2

2. Type the following label in F2 and F3:

   % of Total
   This Month

The formula you want to create for this column will take the total for this month and divide it into each monthly individual total for each of the products. The cell addresses used in the formula will be those for each product that will change, and the Total Amount for all Products this Month, which will not change since it appears only one time in Cell C21.

In a formula, dollar signs are used to indicate an absolute address.

3. Move to Cell F8

4. Type the formula to compute the % of Total:

   +C8/C21 (Ignore the currency format. You will change it later)

5. Press **Enter**

When this formula is copied, the cell C8 will be relative (it will change when copied to a new cell address); the cell C21 is absolute (it will not change when copied so the divisor will always be the value in C21).

You can also use mixed addresses that contain combinations of cell and row locations with a single dollar sign. Examples are: $C19 (locks Column C but allows the row to change), C$19 (locks the row but allows the column to change). You will use mixed addressing in an exercise at the end of this section.

6. Copy this formula individually from **F8** to each of the following cells:

   F11
   F14
   F17
   F19

   Type /**C** for Copy (1-2-3) or CopyRan (Joe)

NOTE: You must use the copy command for each individual cell so that zeroes (0s) are not entered into the cells without values.

To Use the Move Command

You can move the data in a cell or range of cells from one location to another. When you give the MOVE command, you will delete the cell contents from their original location and insert them in the new location.

Suppose, for example, that you wanted to move the values of Column F of your worksheet over a column so that you could insert an additional heading and figures in Column F.

For practice,

1. Move to Cell F8

2. Type /**M** for Move (1-2-3) or MoveRan (Joe)

3. Type the range to move from. For this example, type

   F2..F19

4. Press **Enter**

5. Type the range to move to:

   G2

6. Press **Enter**

NOTE: You need to enter only the first cell of the location to which you are moving—the starting point. The remainder of the cells designated in the range will automatically follow.

To Point to Set a Range

You can also point to the cell(s) to which you want to move (or which you want to copy). The following steps will direct you to restore the column you just moved to its original location.

1. Move to Cell G2

2. Type **/M** for Move (1-2-3) or MoveRan (Joe)

When the “from range” prompt appears, you'll use the period(.) key to lock the beginning of the range.

3. Press **period**

4. Press the **Down Arrow** key to move to G19

NOTE: As you move, the cell location in the command line changes, and the entire cell range is highlighted on the worksheet.

5. Press **Enter**

The “target range” prompt appears.

6. Move to Cell F2 and press **Enter**

The range is back in its original location.

7. Save and replace the DOC2 worksheet again

To Finish the Worksheet

As a review of writing formulas and copying them, complete your worksheet following these step-by-step instructions.

1. Create the following formulas:

In Cell:	Formula:
D8	+C8-B8
E8	+D8/B8

2. Copy the formulas:

In Cell:	Individually to Cells:
D8	D11, D14, D17, D19
E8	E11, E14, E17, E19

To change the format from currency to percent:

1. Move to Cell E8

2. Type **/RFP;** press **Enter** (to accept 2 decimal places)

3. Type **E8..E19** as the range

4. Save and replace the worksheet again

To print the worksheet:

1. Type **/PPR** for Print Printer (1-2-3) or Printer_output (Joe) Range (1-2-3) or Range_to_print (Joe)

2. To enter your range, type **A1..F19**

3. Press **Enter**

4. Be sure the printer is ready and then press **G** for Go

5. Press **Q** to quit the command mode

NOTE: Negative values appear in spreadsheet cells in a format typically used by accountants. Negative numbers are enclosed in parentheses. For example, the value of D14 is ($437.58), indicating that the result of calculating the formula is a negative number.

To Insert or Delete Rows or Columns

Inserting and deleting are both done through the Worksheet (or WorkSets) command.

To insert a row:

1. Move to Cell A2

The new row will be inserted at the cursor position. This blank row will be inserted between the main heading and the subheadings.

2. Press **/WIR** for Worksheet Insert Row (1-2-3) or WorkSets Insert Row (Joe)

3. Press **Enter**

NOTE: You may also insert more than one row. After choosing Row, you can type a range of rows you would like to be blank. You do not need to worry about entering a horizontal range since the Row insert automatically affects the entire width of the worksheet.

To insert three blank rows above the total row:

4. Move to the start of the Total row, A22

5. Type **/WIR**

6. To indicate the range of added rows, type **A22..A24**

7. Press **Enter**

The Total row is pushed down on the worksheet.

To insert a column:

To insert a column between Columns D and E, you will follow the same steps as in the preceding activity, except this time you will choose Column rather than Row.

1. Move to Cell E1

2. Type **/WIC** for Worksheet Insert Column (1-2-3) or WorkSets Insert Column (Joe)

3. Press **Enter**

As with rows, you could type a range of new columns if you wished to add more than one blank column to your worksheet.

To delete columns or rows:

You can delete extra rows or columns the same way you inserted them. The only change in the command you give will be to substitute Delete for Insert. The position of your highlight will indicate the row to delete.

1. Move to Cell E1 (at the top of the column just added)

NOTE: You could be anywhere in the column. You could also be at another location in the worksheet, in which case you would enter the row to be deleted.

2. Type **/WDC** for Worksheet Delete Column (1-2-3) or WorkSets Delete Column_delete (Joe)

3. Press **Enter**

To delete the four added rows, A18..A22, this time type the range after choosing R for Rows (1-2-3) or Row_delete (Joe).

4. Type **/WDR**

5. To indicate range to be deleted, type **A22..A24**

6. Press **Enter**

To Create Separator Lines

Business reports often use separator lines to neatly separate elements such as titles from the main body, or to separate a total line from the figures above it. These lines usually consist of a string of dashes reaching from the left column to the right column of the worksheet.

1. Move to Cell A21

Add a separator line just above the Total line, using the spreadsheet's repeat function. To do this, you'll use the backslash (\) and hyphen (-) characters.

2. Type \ and press **Enter**

The backslash command tells the program that you want the entire cell to be filled with the next character. In this case, the following character is a hyphen (-).

Now all you need to do is copy this cell to the remaining cells in this row of your worksheet, in this case, Cells B21 through F21.

1. Type **/C** for Copy (1-2-3) or Copy_Ran (Joe) and press **Enter** at the "From:" prompt

2. At the "To" prompt, specify the appropriate range, by typing **B22..F22**

3. Press **Enter**

A row of dashes appears above the Total line.

4. Type **/FS** and press **Enter** to save the file

5. Then press **R** to Replace the earlier version

Review Questions on Exercise 3.7

1. State the difference between a relative and absolute address in a formula.

2. What is the command for copying one cell's contents to another cell or range of cells?

3. What is the command for moving a cell's contents to a new location on the worksheet?

4. How are rows or columns inserted? How are they deleted?

5. What is the command used to repeat a character?

Answers to the Review Questions on Exercise 3.7

1. In a relative address the cell locations change to match those in the range to which they are copied. An absolute cell address keeps the cell location the same regardless of where it is moved.
2. /C Enter range to copy from, Enter range to copy to.
3. /M Enter range to copy from, Enter range to copy to.
4. (Part 1) /WI (C or R) Enter
   (Part 2) /WD (C or R) Enter
5. \ (backslash) - (hyphen) Enter

PRESENTATION GRAPHICS

PREVIEW

It's a well-known fact that people can assimilate information faster if it's presented to them in picture form. So it's not surprising that one of a spreadsheet's most popular features is its ability to rapidly develop presentation-quality graphs from worksheet values. In this lesson, you will learn how to use your spreadsheet program to construct, save, and print a bar chart, pie chart, and line chart. See the examples shown on the following pages.

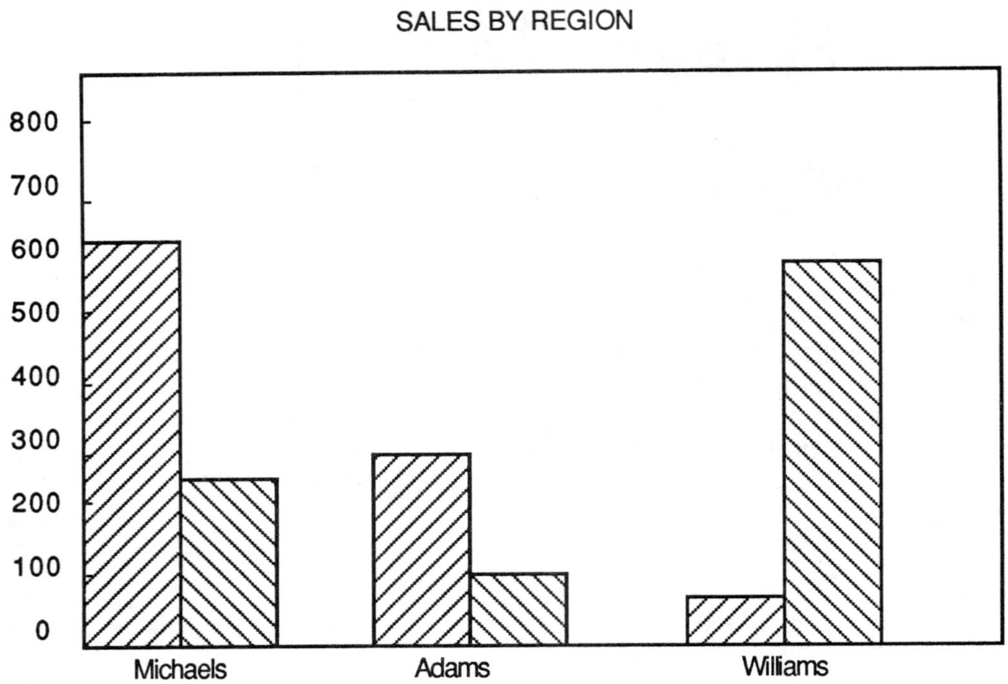

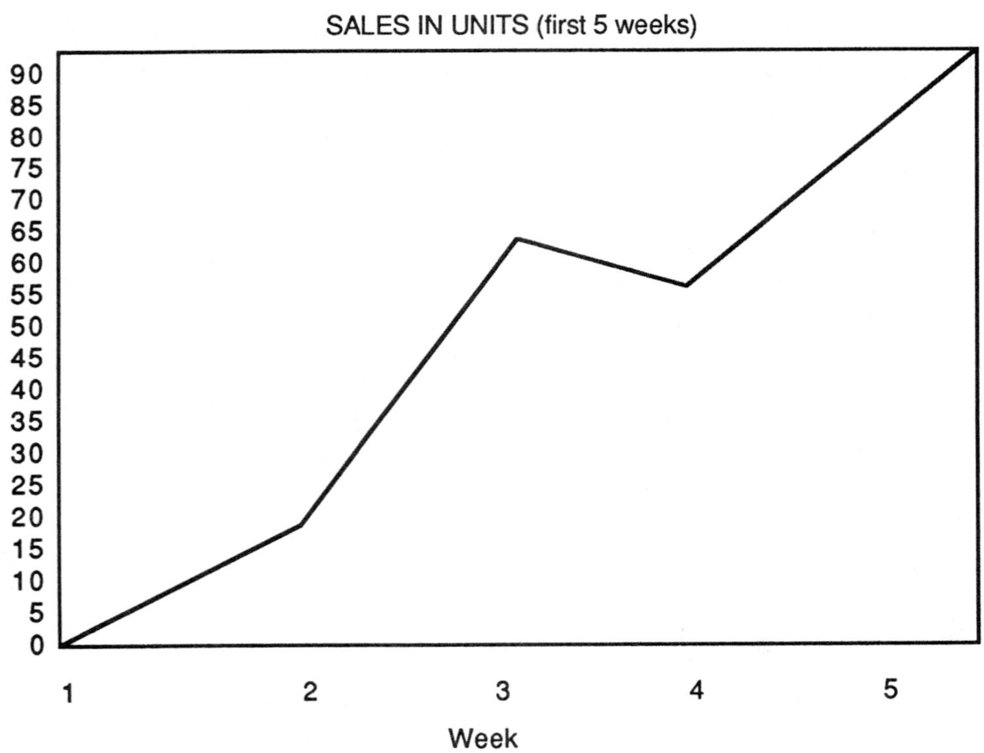

Bar and Line Graphs

(Continued)

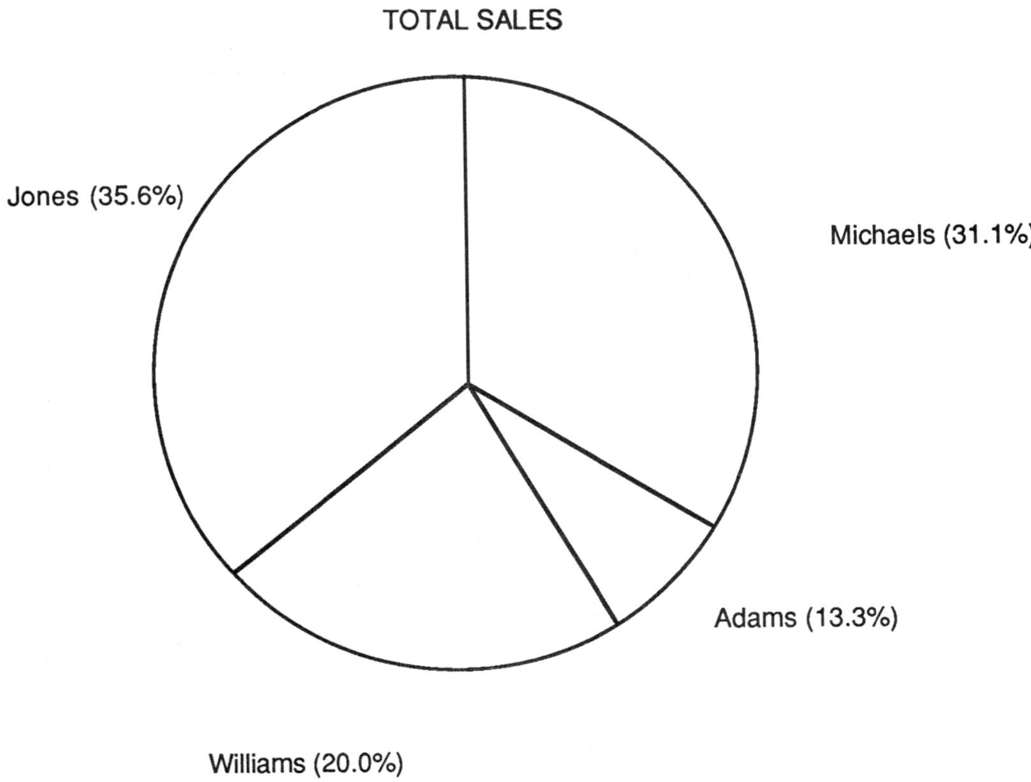

Pie Chart

Figure 3-8. Sample Graphs

Before you begin, you should make sure that your monitor is capable of displaying graphics and that your system unit has a graphics display board. Most monitors sold for the IBM-PC and compatible computers are capable of producing graphics. However, unless your system unit has a graphics display board, and the spreadsheet software knows the graphics environment with which it is dealing, you will not be able to see any graphs on your display screen. Many dot-matrix printers made today support graphics output, but you should check to see that your printer does this before proceeding.

EXERCISE 3.8 HOW TO CREATE GRAPHS

In this exercise you're going to create different types of graphs using the data in the DOC1 worksheet you did in Exercises 3.2 through 3.4.

To Create a Bar Graph

1. To retrieve the worksheet called DOC1, type **/FR**

2. Move the arrow keys to highlight DOC1

3. Type **/G** for Graph

4. Press **T** for Type

The Type command on the submenu summons a list of subcommands. This submenu enables you to choose the type of graph you want.

5. Press **B** for Bar (1-2-3) or Bar_graph (Joe) and press **Enter**

<u>To label the X- and Y-axes:</u>

You are now ready to select the worksheet values and labels that are to be graphed and to tell the spreadsheet where these values or labels are to appear in the graph. Your goal is to produce a bar graph like the one in Figure 3.8, showing each agent's sales for two different regions. To place the names of the sales agents along the graph's horizontal X-axis,

1. Press **X** for X_axis (1-2-3) or X_range (Joe)

from the graph submenu. When the computer prompts you for the X-axis range,

2. Type (or use the pointer method) **A2..A5**

3. Press **Enter**

You are now back at the main graph commands.

4. Press **A**

to identify the values that will be used to graph the leftmost bar for each sales agent (the Region A totals). These values appear in Column B of the worksheet. When the computer prompts you for the first range (or the A range),

5. Type **B2..B5** and press **Enter**

At this time you will return to the main graph submenu.

6. Press **B**

to identify the values for the rightmost bars for each agent in the chart. These bars will show the values contained in Column C of

your worksheet.
When prompted for the second data range,

7. Type **C2..C5** and press **Enter**

The graph is now finished except for the title.

8. Press **O** for Options

from the graph submenu. Both 1-2-3 and Joe let you supply titles of up to two lines.

9. Press **T** for Titles

10. Press **F** for First (1-2-3) or First_title (Joe)

11. Type **SALES BY REGION** and press **Enter**

12. To create the second title, Press **TS** for Second (1-2-3) or Second_title (Joe)

13. Type **January 1991** and press **Enter**

To View the Graph

Now you are ready to view the graph. It is a good idea to view the graph prior to printing so that you can make any necessary adjustments to the graph. To do this,

1. Press **Q** for Quit

At the graph subcommands

2. Press **V** for View

At this point your graph should appear on the screen.

If you wish to change the graph for any reason, reselect any of the graph-command options discussed so far and make the appropriate changes. As usual, you can either type your changes or use the pointer method to make them.

To Save the Graph

When your graph is satisfactory,

1. Press **S** for Save (1-2-3) or **N** for Named_graphs (Joe)

2. In Joe only, press **C** to Create a new named graph

3. Type **DOC1Bar** to indicate the name of this Bar Graph of worksheet DOC1

The spreadsheet package automatically adds the extension .PIC to all saved graphs.

NOTE: When you save a graph, it is not saved permanently until you save the spreadsheet from which you are designing the graph.

To Print the Graph

<u>From 1-2-3 with a dual-disk system:</u>

To print any 1-2-3 graph, you first need to return to the Lotus Access System Menu. Instead of exiting to DOS,

1. Press **P** to choose PrintGraph from the graph submenu

1-2-3 will respond with the message

> Insert Lotus PrintGraph disk in Drive A and
> press [Enter]; press [Esc] to quit

2. Follow the directions and press **Enter**

The main menu of the PrintGraph disk will be pointing to Select

3. Press **S** for Select

The next screen to appear lists the names of the graphs that are saved on the B drive (i.e., those graphs with .PIC extensions). A highlight appears over the top name. Using the Down Arrow key, you can move this highlight to any of the names on the list. As usual, you select the highlighted entry by pressing the Enter key.

Once you've selected the graph to be printed, you'll be returned to the main PrintGraph menu. At this point, first make sure your printer is activated and then

4. Press **G** for Go to print the graph

<u>From 1-2-3 with a hard-disk system:</u>

NOTE: You do not need to return to the Access Menu when using a hard disk.

1. Press **P** for PrintGraph from the graph submenu and be sure the printer is activated

2. Press **G** for Go

From Joe:

You can print out graphs with Joe if you have one of the printers that Joe supports. To print a graph, follow the steps below.

1. To install the printer, type **/WGIP**

2. Press **Shift F10** to print the current graph

To Reset

If you are creating several charts from a single worksheet, you need to Reset the settings prior to creating each chart.

To do this,

1. Type **/GR** for Graph Reset

This command will delete all headings, labels, ranges, etc., from the previous chart so that you may begin with new setups.

To Create Pie Charts

Pie charts are constructed in a manner very similar to bar charts. The primary difference is that a pie chart uses only one range of values. It represents the range values as percentages of a whole.

With the DOC1 worksheet still on the screen,

1. Type **/GTP** for Graph Type Pie (1-2-3) or Pie_graph (Joe)

The procedure to identify the X range and the two-line title for the graph is identical to the corresponding process for bar charts.

2. Press **X** for X_axis or X_range, type **A2..A5** and press **Enter**

3. Identify the A range by pressing **A** and typing **D2..D5** and pressing **Enter**

4. To add a title, type **OTF** and then type the title **TOTAL SALES** and finally press **Enter**

Follow the same steps as with bar charts, to view, save, and print the pie chart.

5. To view it, type **QV** for Quit View

6. To save it, type **S** (1-2-3) or **NC** (Joe) and then type the chart name **DOC1Pie**

7. Follow directions for your system configuration in the preceding section "To Print the Graph"

8. Press **Q** for Quit to return to the READY mode

To Create Line Charts

The procedure for constructing line charts, once you understand how to make bar and pie charts, is simple!

Suppose, for example, that the sales (in units) for a new product in a particular five-week period are as follows:

25 units the first week
45 units the second week
75 units the third week
70 units the fourth week
90 units the fifth week

From these figures you can create a line chart. Your first step is to create a new worksheet containing the figures for each week.

1. Type the labels as follows:

Remember, these are labels, so add an apostrophe in front of each one.

In Cell:	Type:
A1	**'1**
A2	**'2**
A3	**'3**
A4	**'4**
A5	**'5**

2. Type the following values (no apostrophe!):

In Cell:	Type:
B1	**25**
B2	**45**
B3	**75**
B4	**70**
B5	**90**

3. Type / **GTL** for Graph Type Line (1-2-3) or Line_graph (Joe)

When you return to the graph submenu,

4. To identify the X range, press **X** and then type **A1..A5** and finally press **Enter**

5. To identify the A range, press **A** and then type **B1..B5** and finally press **Enter**

To type in a two-line title,

6. Type **OTF** for Options Titles First (1-2-3) or First_title (Joe)

7. Type **SALES IN UNITS** and press **Enter**

8. Type **TS** for Titles Second (1-2-3) or Second_title and then type **(first five weeks)** and press **Enter**

To label the X-axis from the graph submenu,

9. Type **OTX** for Options Titles X-axis

When the spreadsheet package prompts you for the X-axis title,

10. Type **Week** and press **Enter**

To label the Y-axis from the graph submenu,

11. Press **T** for Titles and then press **Y** for Y-axis

When the program prompts you for the Y-axis title

12. Type **Sales** and press **Enter**

At this point, the graph is finished.

13. To view the graph, type **QV** for Quit and View

14. To save the graph, press **S** for Save (1-2-3) or **NC** for Named_graph Create (Joe) and then type the title **DOC3 Line**

15. Print a copy of the line chart following instructions in the preceding section "To Print the Graph"

16. Type **/GR** to reset

17. Press **Q** to quit the graph

18. Type **/FS** for File Save

19. For the worksheet title, type **DOC3** and press **Enter**

20. Type **/Q** to quit the program

PRACTICE DOCUMENTS

The following documents will reinforce the knowledge you have acquired during the exercises up to this point and will also introduce a few additional features that will be useful when doing spreadsheets on your own.

Practice Documents 1 through 3 will reinforce setting up a basic spreadsheet, editing it, copying cells, writing simple formulas, and saving and printing the spreadsheet. Documents 4 through 9 will not only reinforce functions but will also introduce a few new ones with each worksheet.

It is highly recommended that you proceed through each exercise in the order of presentation. The practice presented in each exercise is essential for a better comprehension of the exercise.

PRACTICE DOCUMENT 1

Objectives:

In this exercise, you will practice

a. copying values from cell to cell
b. saving a worksheet
c. retrieving a worksheet
d. printing a worksheet
e. adjusting column width
f. calculating an average
g. making changes to the worksheet
h. creating a formula for subtracting one value from another

1. Prepare the partial worksheet below:

	A	B	C	D	E	F
1	Day	Jan 1	Jan 2	Jan 3	Jan 4	Jan 5
2	Sales	500	800	600	700	800
3	Costs	350	700	150	200	400
4	Profits					
5						
6						

2. Compute profits by taking sales minus costs for each of the days presented. Create a formula for Cell B4 and copy it to other applicable cells in the Profits row.

3. Save the worksheet as PRDOC1 for Practice Document 1

4. Quit the spreadsheet and go to a system prompt

5. Sign on to the program and retrieve the worksheet

6. Print out the worksheet on your printer

Modifications to PRDOC1

1. Adjust the column widths in PRDOC1 as follows:

   a. Column A: 20 characters
   b. Columns B through F: 6 characters

2. Format sales and costs for the entire worksheet in Currency format. Carry the decimal 2 points.

NOTE: The columns now show asterisks (********).

3. Adjust the width of the columns so that all values appear (at least 8 spaces wide)

4. Calculate the average sales, costs, and profits for the 5 days shown in Document 1, placing these values into the 7th column of the worksheet. Create an appropriate column heading, and then Print, Save, and Replace the worksheet again.

5. How would your worksheet change if the January 1 costs were actually $50 instead of $350? Print a copy of a revised worksheet showing the changes.

NOTE: When you change the 350 to 50, you should not enter a dollar sign ($) or a decimal point (.). Enter the value as a whole number, 50, and press Enter. All formatting is done through the format commands.

6. How would the worksheet change if January 3 sales were $90 instead of $600? Print a copy of the revised worksheet showing these changes.

7. Save the worksheet as PRDOC1R (the R is for revised)

PRACTICE DOCUMENT 2

Objectives:

In this exercise, you will practice

a. using the Copy command
b. using the Move command
c. creating separator lines
d. inserting rows

1. Prepare the worksheet that follows. Remember to use an apostrophe as the first character of the column headings in B, C, D, and E. Remember also to format with dollar signs (currency) and not to type them in.

2. Create a formula in Cell B4 to compute a column called "Income" (Revenue minus Expenses). Use a plus sign (+) at the beginning of the formula.

	A	B	C	D	E
1	Quarter	1st	2nd	3rd	4th
2	Revenue	$200	$100	$600	$200
3	Expenses	$130	$50	$100	$300
4	Income				

3. Copy the formula in B4 to other applicable cells (Income in Columns C, D, and E)

4. Use the Move command to move the entire worksheet in this exercise to L7 (Hint: from A1..E4 to L7)

5. Press **F5** to GoTo Cell L7

6. Create separator lines on the worksheet:

   a. insert a new row above Revenue and one above Income
   b. create a separator line by using the Repeat and Copy commands as follows:

   On the new Row 8: in Cells M8 through P8
   On the new Row 11: in Cells M11 through P11

7. Move the worksheet back to A1 and use F5 (GoTo) to relocate to A1

8. Save the worksheet as PRDOC2

9. Print a copy

PRACTICE DOCUMENT 3

Objectives:

In this exercise, you will practice

a. constructing a bar chart
b. saving a graph
c. printing a graph

1. Using data from PRDOC2, construct a bar chart showing Revenue and Expenses for each quarter. Include the following information:

   a. a title as follows:

      INCOME REPORT
      1991

   b. labels on the X-axis for each quarter
   c. values on the Y-axis ranging from 0 to 1,000

      (1) Options from the graph submenu
      (2) Press **S** for Scaling
      (3) Press **Y** for Y_axis or Y_Scaling
      (4) Press **L** for Lower or Lower_bound

          Type **0** and press **Enter**

      (5) Press **U** for Upper or Upper_bound

          Type **1000** and press **Enter**

      (6) Press **Q** for Quit to Graph submenu

2. Save the bar chart as PRDOC3BR

3. Print a copy of the bar chart

4. Save the worksheet as PRDOC3

PRACTICE DOCUMENTS 4 THROUGH 9 INTRODUCTION

In preparing the remaining worksheets in this section, you will learn how to

a. prepare a multi-period budget
b. prepare a check register for income taxes
c. sort data
d. do a frequency distribution

Hints accompany some of the documents. It is important to read the hints thoroughly. They help to explain some new functions that are introduced and are necessary to completing the worksheet. Otherwise, suggestions are given as a part of the instructions. Some of the new functions covered are:

a. Labeling tips (Document 4)
b. Creating templates (Document 5)
c. The range formatting command (Document 5)
d. The data fill command (Document 5)
e. The 1-2-3 and Joe hierarchy of operations (Document 5)
f. Preparing a frequency distribution (Document 6)
g. Mixed cell addressing (Document 7)
h. Sorting data (Document 8)
i. Freezing horizontal and vertical titles (Document 9)
j. The @IF function (Document 9)

PRACTICE DOCUMENT 4: PREPARING A MULTI-PERIOD CASH BUDGET

Objectives:

In this exercise, you will practice

a. filling in a worksheet from supplied data
b. creating formulas
c. saving the worksheet
d. printing the worksheet
e. reworking the worksheet using assumptions
f. positioning values and labels within a column
g. using the F2 key for editing

If asked to identify their most critical spreadsheet operation, many managers would name budgeting. Because budgets involve guesswork about the future, they often have to be recalculated over and over again under a variety of financial assumptions, commonly known as "what ifs." For example, what if sales projections are 10 percent too high (or too low), what if borrowing rates increase 1 or 2 percent, or what if a revenue or expense item is incurred earlier or later than expected?

IMPORTANT NOTE: Here you will prepare the 1991 cash budget for SeaTech Corporation. A partial worksheet is shown on the following page of the various account titles involved, the expected beginning cash balance of $100,000, and the desired quarter-ending cash balances of $125,000, $165,000, $175,000, and $200,000.

Read the hints at the end of this document if you have problems completing the worksheet.

1. Create a worksheet with the following data

(Use an apostrophe in front of the
dashes in Quarters)

	A	B	C	D	E	F
1	SeaTech Corporation -- 1991 Cash Budget					
2			-- Quarters --			
3		1	2	3	4	
4						
5	Beginning cash balance	$100,000				
6						
7	Total receipts					
8						
9	Disbursements:					
10	Payroll					
11	Supplies					
12	Utilities					
13	Services					
14	Taxes					
15	Equipment					
16	Rent					
17						
18	Total disbursements					
19						
20	Ending cash balance	$125,000	$165,000	$175,000	$200,000	

2. Fill in some of the worksheet using the figures above and the following figures (remember to enter whole numbers and format later)

Assume that the beginning cash balance for any quarter is equivalent to the ending cash balance for the previous quarter.

a. Payroll: Payroll is expected to be $30,000 in Quarter 3, reflecting heavy summer employment. All other quarters are expected to be $20,000.

b. Supplies: Supplies generally run about $10,000 for the first three quarters and $15,000 for the 4th quarter.

c. Utilities: Utilities are usually 3 percent of payroll.

d. Services: Services are expected to be $10,000 for Quarter 1; $15,000 for Quarter 2; zero for Quarter 3; and $10,000 for Quarter 4.

e. Taxes: Taxes will be constant at $20,000 per quarter.

f. Equipment: Expected equipment purchases are $10,000 in Quarter 2; $25,000 in Quarter 3; and $40,000 in Quarter 4.

g. Rent: Rent will be constant at $12,000 per quarter.

So far you should have formulas for the following:

Utilities: to compute 3% of payroll

3. Compute the Total receipts that will be needed in each quarter to cover expenses and to produce the required ending cash balances (as stated in the IMPORTANT NOTE at the beginning of this exercise). Use a formula for this computation. (HINT: Use an @SUM formula to take the ending balance plus the total disbursements minus the beginning balance. Use cell addresses and copy the formula to the appropriate cells.)

4. Save the worksheet as PRDOC4

5. Print a copy of the completed worksheet

6. Rework the computations in Step 2 under the assumption that payroll and services will each be 10 percent higher in 1991

7. Save the modified worksheet as PRDOC4R

8. Print a copy of the revised version

9. Rework the computations from Step 3 again under the assumption that taxes will be 25 percent lower and that equipment purchases will occur a quarter earlier than expected

HINTS: The title in Row 1 is created by moving to Cell A1 then pressing the spacebar several times, and then entering the title. When you enter this label onto the worksheet, you will notice that it spans several columns. If, when you complete the worksheet, the title isn't centered to your satisfaction, use the edit function key (F2) to insert or remove blank spaces.

The Quarters heading in Row 2 is created similarly, starting in Cell D2.

Each of the quarters in Row 3 is centered in its respective column. This is done by placing a label prefix before the label. The prefixes you can use are:

Character:	Action taken:
'	Left justifies
^	Centers
"	Right justifies
\	Repeats

In Row 3 each of the Quarter labels should be entered as

^1
^2

and so forth.

PRACTICE DOCUMENT 5: COMPUTING A DEPRECIATION SCHEDULE

<u>Objectives:</u>

In this exercise, you will practice

a. creating formulas for depreciation
b. adjusting column width
c. centering data within cells
d. using the automatic number generator
e. formatting ranges
f. formatting values
g. changing figures in the worksheet for "what if" speculations

This exercise shows you how to compute a depreciation schedule. The straight-line depreciation method computes annual depreciation expenses by the formula below:

$$\text{Annual depreciation} = \frac{\text{Original cost - Salvage value}}{\text{Useful life}}$$

The straight-line depreciation schedule below represents an asset that originally cost $7,328 and is worth $600 at the end of its 10-year useful life. You will create these amounts through formulas.

	A	B	C	D	E	F	G
1		TEN-YEAR ASSET DEPRECIATION SCHEDULE					
2							
3			Original cost		$7,328.00		
4			Salvage value		$600.00		
5							
6	------------	------------	------------	------------	------------	------------	------------
7	YEAR		DEPRECIATION		ACCUMULATED		UNDEPRECIATED
8			CHARGE		DEPRECIATION		BALANCE
9							
10	1		672.80		672.80		$6,655.20
11	2		$672.80		$1,345.60		$5,982.40
12	3		$672.80		$2,018.40		$5,309.60
13	4		$672.80		$2,691.20		$4,636.80
14	5		$672.80		$3,364.00		$3,964.00
15	6		$672.80		$4,036.80		$3,291.20
16	7		$672.80		$4,709.60		$2,618.40
17	8		$672.80		$5,382.40		$1,945.60
18	9		$672.80		$6,055.20		$1,272.80
19	10		$672.80		$6,728.00		$600.00
20							

To Set Up the Worksheet

1. Type the main heading starting in Column B, and let it overlap into the other columns

2. Center the headings Original Cost and Salvage Value in Cells C3 and C4

3. Enter the headings: YEAR (Column A)

   DEPRECIATION CHARGE (Column C)

   ACCUMULATED DEPRECIATION (Column E)

   UNDEPRECIATED BALANCE (Column G)

   centered under each of the columns using the same label prefixes as those shown at the end of the instructions for Document 4

4. Enter the years using the following automatic number generator:

   a. Type **/DF** for Data Fill (1-2-3) or Database Fill_range (Joe)

   In response to the prompts that appear, type:

   b. **A10..A19** as the fill range
   c. **1** to Start
   d. **1** to Step
   e. **10** to Stop

This series of steps (b through e) tells the spreadsheet program that you want a pattern of numbers that starts with 1, ends with 10, and counts (steps) in units of 1.

5. Repeat the automatic numbering system for the Depreciation Charge amount of $672.80, which is consistent in Cells C10 through C19. (Start and Stop at the same number [672.80] and Step at zero [0].)

Formatting:

Format the dollar amounts (not the years) to include dollar signs.

1. Type **/RE** for Range (1-2-3) or RangeOps (Joe) Format

2. Choose the Currency option and set 2 decimal places

3. Type **C10..G19** and press **Enter** in response to the "Range to format" prompt

NOTE: You may need to widen some of the columns to get the new formats to fit.

<u>Formulas:</u>

1. Create the accumulated depreciation formula for Cell E10. Be sure the original cost value and the salvage value are inserted in Cells E3 and E4 respectively. This formula is computed using the following format:

   (the original cost minus salvage value)/10

   (in Cell E10)

   (original cost minus salvage value)/10 + E10

   (in Cells E11..E19)

HINT: Be sure to create a formula that includes the parentheses. Remember that the values within the parentheses will be computed first. This is critical to the correct working of the formula. Also remember that the cells in E3 and E4 must be absolute so that they do not change when copied. The cell addresses in the formula in E11, however, are relative—they should change.

2. Copy the accumulated depreciation formula to other applicable cells in the Accumulated Depreciation column

3. Create a formula to compute the undepreciated balance:

   The original cost minus the accumulated depreciation

4. Copy the formula in Cell G10 to other applicable cells

5. Save the final worksheet as PRDOC5

6. Print a copy of the worksheet

Modifications to the Worksheet

1. Redo the worksheet for an asset with an original cost of $11,000 and a salvage value of $1,000

2. Save the worksheet again as PRDOC5R

3. Print a copy of the worksheet

PRACTICE DOCUMENT 6: PREPARING A FREQUENCY DISTRIBUTION

Objectives:

In this exercise, you will practice

a. setting up the format for a frequency distribution
b. using the GoTo command
c. using a scratchpad for entering values
d. using the Data or Database Distribution command

Suppose that in your statistics class you have been asked to prepare a frequency distribution of a class's test scores. Twenty-five people took an exam; the scores were distributed as follows:

91, 83, 69, 35, 99, 64, 78, 71, 52, 89, 72, 100, 56, 63, 72, 77, 82, 95, 85, 71, 66, 54, 63, 0, 5

Your professor would like you to prepare a simple table for output in the following format:

Range	Number of Scores in Range
90-100	?
80-89	?
and so forth	

One part of the worksheet in this exercise will need to be reserved for scratchpad computations; another part, for the desired output. Because 1-2-3 and Joe allow you to print only a portion (range) of the worksheet, you will be printing only the output portion. The scratchpad will be developed in a remote part of the worksheet and will not be used for output.

Both parts of the worksheet are shown in the following example. The output section is on the left; the scratchpad is on the right.

	A	B
1	FREQUENCY	
2		
3	Range	Number of
4		Scores
5		
6	90-100	4
7	80-89	4
8	70-79	6
9	60-69	5
10	50-59	3
11	40-49	0
12	30-39	1
13	20-29	0
14	10-19	0
15	0-9	2
16		
17		
18		
19		
20		
21		
22		

	I	J	K	L
1		Scratchpad Computations		
2				
3	Score		Bin	Frequency
4	91		9	2
5	83		19	0
6	69		29	0
7	35		39	1
8	99		49	0
9	64		59	3
10	78		69	5
11	71		79	6
12	52		89	4
13	89		100	4
14	72			0
15	100			
16	56			
17	63			
18	72			
19	77			
20	82			
21				
22				

Column I above shows only the first 17 scores. You'll need to enter the rest of the scores in that column.

Column K contains bins, which you set up. The "9" (Cell K4) catches all scores less than or equal to 9, the 19 (Cell K5) catches all scores greater than 9 but less than or equal to 19. You can see that these boundaries are also shown in the Range column in Column A. Starting from the bottom the same numbers appear: 9, 19, 29, etc.

With this column set up, the program will know that it is searching for the frequency of numbers falling within this range.

Column L shows the frequencies for all 25 scores. This column will receive the number of observations within each bin.

Here are the steps you follow to create this worksheet.

1. Move to Cell A1 and type **FREQUENCY**

2. Type the following labels in the cells indicated:

   Range (A3)
   Number of (B3)
   Scores (B4)

3. Type the ranges shown in Cells A6 through A15 as labels (use an apostrophe as the first character of each label that starts with a digit)

4. Move to Cell J1 (use the GoTo command) and type the label **Scratchpad Computations**

5. Then type these labels in the cells indicated:

   Score (I3)
   Bin (K3)
   Frequency (L3)

6. Enter the 25 scores listed at the start of this exercise in Cells I4 through I28

7. Enter the values for the Bins in Cells K4 through K13

8. Move to Cell L4

9. To calculate bin frequencies,
   a. Type **/DD** for Data (1-2-3) or Database (Joe) Distribution
   b. In response to the prompt "Enter values range," type **I4..I28** and press **Enter**
   c. In response to the prompt "Enter bin range," type **K4..K13** and press **Enter**

The frequencies that will be calculated are shown in Column L. The zero at the bottom of the column is giving the information that there were no scores greater than 100.

You now need to transfer the frequencies in Column L to Column B. You'll notice from the example that Column B shows the scores in reverse, beginning with the highest range. You can have the program insert the scores by entering a formula.

10. Move to Cell B6 and type the formula **+L13**

11. Move to Cell B7 and type the formula **+L12**

12. Continue entering formulas in each cell as follows:

    B8: **+L11**
    B9: **+L10**
    B10: **+L9**
    B11: **+L8**
    B12: **+L7**
    B13: **+L6**
    B14: **+L5**
    B15: **+L4**

The scores are inserted in the cells in Column B.

13. Save the worksheet as PRDOC7

14. Print a copy of the output of the worksheet (Columns A and B)

PRACTICE DOCUMENT 7: MIXED-CELL ADDRESSING

Objectives:

In this exercise, you will practice creating a formula to compute future sums, using

a. addition
b. multiplication
c. exponentiation
d. mixed-cell addressing

Formatting a Range of Values

This is a good exercise for practicing mixed-cell addressing. As you learned earlier in this section, 1-2-3 and Joe can copy the contents of a cell in either a relative (the cell location[s] used in the formula adjusts to the cell[s] copied to) or absolute (dollar signs are used to "fix" the cell position in the formula so that it does not change when copied) way. There are many times, however, when you might want to mix these copying schemes; for example, when keeping a row value fixed while varying column values. You learned earlier that this is mixed-cell addressing.

Many tables, such as the one you will set up here, require some form of mixed-cell addressing. In the present case, this will allow you to write the interest-rate formula used and copy it to other cells.

Partial output of the table you will produce is shown below:

	A	B	C	D	E	F
1			Future Sum Computations			
2						
3	Years	10.0%	10.5%	11.0%	11.5%	12.0%
4	1	1.1	1.105	1.11	1.115	1.12
5	2	1.21	1.221025	1 .2321	1.243225	1.2544
6	3	1.331	1.349232	1.367631	1.386195	1.404928
7	4	.				
8	5	.				
9	6	.				
10	7	.				
11	8	.				
12	9	.				
13	10	2.593742	2.714080	2.839420	2.969946	3.105848

In this example, P dollars are invested in an account today at a compounded interest rate of R percent per period; the amount of the account at the end of N periods is given by the formula:

$$S = P(1+R/100)^N$$

The table shows the value of $1 at the end of 1, 2, 3,....,10 years at interest rates of 10, 10.5, 11, 11.5, and 12 percent.

For this table, you will need to create only one formula. That formula will then be copied to all other cells.

1. Create the worksheet shown here by entering the following labels:

   a. The centered heading, Future Sum Computations
   b. All labels in Row 3 (this time enter the percentage column headings as values and format them as percents)
   c. The years in Column A (as values!)

2. Create the following formula for Cell B4:

   @SUM(1+B$3)^$A4

Notice how this formula corresponds to the formula, $S=P(1+R/100)^N$.

You are taking the $1 value (your original investment), adding it to the rate (across Row 3) and carrying it to the power of the number of years (down Column A).

This formula also tells 1-2-3 and Joe that you always want the rate value taken from Row 3 and the year value taken from Column A. Those values must remain constant so dollar signs are placed in front of the 3 and the A in the formula. Everything else is relative to the row and column into which you are copying. When you copy this formula across to another column or down to another row, the program will always keep 3 and A intact.

3. Copy the formula from B4 to all other applicable cells in the worksheet (B4..F13)

Take time to look at the changes in the formula in other cells both down the rows and across the columns.

4. Save the worksheet as PRDOC7

5. Print a copy of the worksheet

PRACTICE DOCUMENT 8: SORTING DATA AND FREEZING TITLES

<u>Objectives:</u>

In this exercise, you will practice

a. using Data Sort or Database Sort to sort labels and values
b. doing Primary key sorts
c. freezing horizontal and vertical titles

You have been asked by one of your professors to set up a grade book.

To Create the Worksheet

1. Create the partial gradebook as shown below, adjusting column widths as necessary:

	A	B	C	D	E	F
1			Computer Information Systems 101			
2			Grade Book			
3			Fall Semester, 1991			
4			Professor Rufus J. Flywheel, Ph.D.			
5						
6						
7						
8	----------------	----------------	----------------	----------------	----------------	----------------
9	Student name	Exam 1	Exam 2	Exam 3	Exam 4	Average
10	Zinn, Fred	85	81	76	74	
11	Smith, Abel	55	76	88	46	
12	Edwards, Frank	75	98	87	92	
13	Rourke, Patricia	93	87	99	98	
14						

2. Continue entering the names of students and their scores as follows:

Gonzales, Jesus: 87, 94, 94, 75
Telzer, Marta: 66, 75, 78, 65
Robertson, Joe: 76, 81, 88, 92
Lyons, Katrina: 85, 83, 92, 88
Pritchard, C. J.: 65, 71, 68, 82
Littledog, Cyrus: 75, 85, 97, 86
Simon, Susanne: 76, 88, 85, 72
Lewis, Bobbi: 65, 72, 75, 79
Wiggins, Percy: 84, 94, 85, 93
Williams, Van: 76, 58, 89, 84
Haji, Ali: 82, 89, 94, 86
Yazzie, Mary: 82, 97, 88, 75
Davidson, Norm: 76, 81, 75, 67
Lindstrom, Per: 88, 65, 82, 79

Martin, Liz: 66, 65, 74, 78
Barton, Mike: 76, 56, 67, 81

To Sort the Worksheet

1. Sort the worksheet by typing **/DSD** for Data (1-2-3) or Database (Joe) Sort Data sort_range

2. Type the range **A10..E13**

3. Press **Enter**

4. Press **P** for Primary-key or Primary_sort_key

5. Because you want to sort names alphabetically, type **A10..A29** and press **Enter** to indicate the range of name listings

6. In response to the "Sort order" prompt, press **A** for Ascending and press **Enter**

7. To start the sort, press **G** for Go or Go_sort

The spreadsheet program sorts the names in Column A in ascending order.

NOTE: Both 1-2-3 and Joe also allow you to identify a "secondary key" (column), which will allow you to do sorts within a sort. For example, if your records for each student had a "majors" column (showing whether a student was majoring in accounting, finance, marketing, or some other field), you might want to sort the records first on the majors column (the primary key) and then on the name column (the secondary key). When you make changes to the worksheet, you can save the individual worksheets under different names and have a copy of each.

To Freeze the Horizontal Titles

Freezing titles enables you to keep titles and margin headings fixed on the screen as you scroll or page through the data on the worksheet. In the current, 28-name example, it will allow you to keep the titles and column headings in Rows 1-9 fixed. To do this,

1. Place the highlight anywhere in Line 8 and type **/WTH** for Worksheet or WorkSets Titles Horizontal or Horizontal_titles

2. Use the PgDn and PgUp keys to flip forward and backward through the data records. You can also use the

Up Arrow and Down Arrow cursor-movement keys to scroll a record at a time.

To Freeze the Vertical Titles

1. Place the highlight in Cell B9 (to freeze the titles to the left of that column)

2. Type **/WTV** for Worksheet or WorkSets Titles Vertical or Vertical_titles

The titles in Column A are frozen.

3. Move to the right with the Tab key or the arrow keys and back again. Notice how the titles stay frozen.

4. Insert three additional blank columns to the left of the Average column

5. Add these headings to the new columns: Exam 5 (Column F), Exam 6 (Column G), and Exam 7 (Column H). Add a vertical separator line to the right of Column H.

6. Scroll to the right until you are immediately to the right of the names and aligned under Exam 5 (Cell F10)

7. Add the following scores for each of the students by pressing the Tab key or the Right Arrow key to move from left to right (the scores are ready to be added in alphabetical order from the top, beginning with Barton):

   80,54,78
   85,75,84
   90,73,81
   95,80,75
   75,90,82
   82,90,78
   67,80,80
   78,91,74
   90,82,86
   78,65,75
   92,83,76
   59,80,78
   89,95,90
   82,75,89
   75,83,78
   78,87,87
   72,72,100
   89,82,85
   95,92,90
   94,82,74

When the vertical labels are frozen, notice how much easier it is to determine whom the scores belong to.

You can also set both of the titles at once by typing **/WTB** for Worksheet or WorkSets Titles Both or Both_left_and_above

To Clear the Title Lock

1. Type **/WTC** for Worksheet or WorkSets Titles Clear or Clear_titles

2. Save the worksheet as PRDOC8

3. Print a copy of the worksheet

PRACTICE DOCUMENT 9: PREPARING A CHECK REGISTER

Objectives:

In this exercise, you will practice

- a. writing IF functions
- b. creating IF functions to test conditions in multiple columns

Most businesses, especially around tax time, need to pore over the checks they have written and determine which expenses fall into each of several expense categories. Take KM Company, for instance. They were able to prepare the check register and expense summary below, showing all of the checks paid out in the first quarter of 1991.

	A	B	C	D	E	F
1					Summary of Expenses	
2		**********************************			1=Rent $2,100	
3		KM COMPANY			2=Supp. $60	
4		FIRST QUARTER CHECK SUMMARY			3=Util. $180	
5		**********************************			4=Serv. $750	
6					5=D.A. $1,600	
7	----------	----------	----------	----------	----------	----------
8	Check No.	Date		Paid To	Amount	Code
9	1503	187		XYZ Enterprises	$700	1
10	1509	287		XYZ Enterprises	$700	1
11	1499	187		Ace Suppliers	$45	2
12	1511	387		BZ Power and Elect.	$60	3
13	1510	287		Linda Smith Services	$400	4
14	1506	187		Larson's	$900	5
15	1504	187		Dave's Warehouse	$700	5
16	1505	187		BZ Power and Elect.	$55	3
17	1496	187		Ellis Services	$350	4
18	1502	187		Ace Suppliers	$15	2
19	1508	287		BZ Power and Elect.	$65	3
20	1512	387		XYZ Enterprise	$700	1
21						

To calculate the "Summary of Expenses," you'll set up IF functions that evaluate each expense's code and add its amount to the correct category.

1. Begin by filling in all cells, A1 through D20 and E8 through F20 as shown above. Adjust cell width as necessary. (Don't forget that labels starting with a digit, such as those in Columns A and B, must start with an apostrophe [']. Also, enter the amounts in Column E without the dollar sign and then format them for currency.)

2. Move to Cell G8 and type **Rent**

Type the following labels in the indicated cells:

Supp. in H8
Util. in I8
Serv. in J8
D.A. in K8

3. Type the following function in Cell G9:

@IF(F9=1,E9,0)

This function reads as follows: If the value found in F9 equals 1 (or Code 1) then insert the amount found in E9 into this cell. Otherwise insert a zero.

Since you are presently in the column for Category 1, any Code 1 found will be inserted.

4. Type the following functions in the specified cells:

@IF(F9=2,E9,0) in H9
@IF(F9=3,E9,0) in I9
@IF(F9=4,E9,0) in J9
@IF(F9=5,E9,0) in K9

5. Copy each of the functions down its respective column. Because the functions are all relative (containing no dollar signs), the cell location will change as you copy so that the function in H10 will read:

@IF(F10=1,E10,0)
.... and so on

In this way the program will always be looking for conditions that exist in the current row.

6. Move to Cell E1 and type **Summary of Expenses**

7. Type the following labels in the cells indicated, starting each with an apostrophe:

'1=Rent in E2
'2=Supp. in E3
'3=Util. in E4
'4=Serv. in E5
'5=D.A. in E6

8. To calculate the expense code totals for the Summary, type the following functions in the specified cells:

Function:	Type in Cell:
@SUM(G9..G20)	F2
@SUM(H9..H20)	F3
@SUM(I9..I20)	F4
@SUM(J9..J20)	F5
@SUM(K9..K20)	F6

9. Format the values in cell F2 through F6 for currency

10. Save the worksheet as PRDOC9

11. Print a copy of the output range: A1 through F20

COMMAND SUMMARY

This section briefly summarizes many of the most-used functions of 1-2-3 and Joe. This section is meant to be used only as a reference after completing the full 1-2-3 and Joe instructions contained in the preceding exercises.

Addresses—Absolute

When moving or copying a formula from one cell to other cells, dollar signs are included in the formula so that cell locations remain absolute (do not change).

Example:

@SUM(A6..C3)

Wherever this function is copied, the location of Cell C3 will remain the same.

Addresses—Relative

When a formula (or function) is moved or copied to other cells, cell coordinates in the formula automatically change relative to their new cell location.

Example:

a formula written as +B2+B5 in Cell B7 will change to +C2+C5 when copied to C7

Column Width—Adjusting

1. Type **/WCS**
2. Type in the new width
3. Press **Enter**

Copying

1. Type **/C**
2. Enter the range to copy from
3. Enter the range to copy to

4. Press **Enter**

Default—Setting

With a hard disk and 1-2-3:

1. Type **/DA:**

2. Press **Enter**

With a dual-disk system and 1-2-3 or Joe:

1. Type **/DB:**

2. Press **Enter**

With a hard disk and Joe:

1. Type **/WGDD Esc A:**

2. Press **Enter**

3. Type **UQ**

Editing Cells

With the F2 key:

1. Move to the cell to be edited

2. Press **F2**

3. Move with the arrow keys and use the delete key and/or type the values or labels to be added

4. Press **Enter**

In the worksheet:

You may edit cells by entering new contents into the cell. The old values or labels are then deleted.

You may also highlight the cell whose contents you want to delete and

1. Type **/R**
2. Press **Enter** when the cell location is highlighted, or enter a cell range to erase

Format—Global Settings

1. Type **/WGF**
2. Select the type of format wanted
3. Type the number of desired decimal places
4. Press **Enter**

Format—Range Settings

1. Type **/RF**
2. Choose the type of format
3. Set the decimal places
4. Press **Enter**

Formulas

Formulas direct the program to perform one or more calculations involving the values in specified cells. A formula always begins with +. (Also see "Operators.") Example of a formula:

+B8.D23	to divide the value in B8 by the value in D23

Functions

Functions are predefined calculations performed on the values in a range of cells. A function always begins with @. Examples of functions are:

@SUM(B4..B11)	to add the values in B4 through B11
@AVG(C12..C42)	to calculate the average of the values in Cells C12 through C42

Graphs—Creating

1. Type **/GT**
2. Choose type of graph

<u>To label the x and y axis:</u>

1. Type **X** or **Y** (from the graph submenu)

2. Enter the range for the X axis or Y axis

3. Press **Enter**

To identify data ranges:

1. Choose one letter (A, B, C, etc.) from the graph submenu to identify each data range to be used

2. Type the range of values for that data range

3. Press **Enter**

4. Repeat the first three steps choosing a different letter for each data range needed

To set titles:

1. Type **OTF**

2. Type the first title for the top of the graph

3. Press **Enter**

4. Type **TS** to add a second title

5. Type the second title

6. Press **Enter**

Graphs—Printing

With a dual-disk system and 1-2-3:

1. Press **P** for Print Graph on the graph submenu

2. Follow instructions for inserting the PrintGraph diskette

3. Press **Enter**

4. Press **S** to select the graph you want to print

5. Highlight the graph to be printed

6. Press **Enter**

7. Press **G** for Go

With a hard disk and 1-2-3:

1. Press **P** for PrintGraph

2. Press **G** for Go

With Joe:

Press the **Alt** and **F10** keys to print the current graph; press the **Shift** and **F10** keys to print a named graph you have selected

Graphs—Resetting

It is necessary to reset if you are making several graphs from a single worksheet. Resetting erases all previous settings.

Type **/GR** to reset

Graphs—Saving

In 1-2-3:

1. Press **S**
2. Type the graph name

In Joe:

1. Press **NC**
2. Type the graph name

Graphs—Viewing

1. Press **Q** for Quit
2. Press **V** for View

Installing the Printer

With Joe only:

1. Type **/WGDIP**
2. Select your printer from the options
3. Press **Enter**
4. Press **Q**

Moving

1. Type /**M**
2. Enter the range to move from
3. Press **Enter**
4. Enter the range to move to
5. Press **Enter**

Operators

Operators appear in formulas and direct the program to do a specific calculation. The operators in 1-2-3 and Joe are:

^ exponentiation
* multiplication
/ division
+ addition
- subtraction

The hierarchy of the operators is as follows:

a. exponentiation is performed first
b. multiplication and division are performed next, in the order in which they occur
c. addition and subtraction are performed last, in the order in which they occur

Pointing to a Range

Whenever you are setting a range, you can use the arrow keys to set the last cell location in the range.

1. Type /**M** for Move
2. Press **Enter** (to lock the beginning range)
3. Press the Down or Right Arrow keys to move to the last cell in the range
4. Press **Enter**
5. Type in the cell of the target location
6. Press **Enter**

Printing the Worksheet

1. Type **/PPR**

2. Enter the range of cells to print

3. Press **G**

4. Press **Q** to quit the menu

Retrieving a File

1. Type **/FR**

2. Type the name of the file to retrieve or highlight the filename from the list

3. Press **Enter**

Rows and Columns—Deleting

1. Type **/WD**

2. Press **R** for rows or press **C** for columns

3. Enter range

4. Press **Enter**

Rows and Columns—Inserting

1. Type **/WI**

2. Press **R** for rows or **C** for columns

3. Enter range

4. Press **Enter**

Saving the Worksheet

1. Type **/F**

2. Type the name of the worksheet if this is the first time it has been saved

3. Press **Enter**

Separator Lines—Creating

Separator lines on the worksheet are formed from a series of hyphens (-). The backslash (\) is the repeat function used to replicate the hyphen.

1. Position the cell pointer where you want the line to start

2. Type \-

3. Press **Enter**

4. Type /C

5. Type the cell range where you want the line copied to

6. Press **Enter**

NOTES

SECTION 4

DATABASE

PREVIEW

One of the major problems businesses face is that of storing, managing, and accessing large amounts of data for their everyday operations. Information from data is used to make decisions about what products to sell, to review accounts payable, and to prepare payroll reports. It is used to study what is happening with the inventory on hand and to answer many questions that arise in day-to-day business operations.

There are many ways in which you maintain data and later gather information from it. For example, you may have a drawer in which you save graded papers from all of your classes. You may go through these data from time to time to gather information, such as what scores you've received so far this term in a particular class or how your scores this term compare with last term. You might make a list of your scores in a class and compute your current grade average.

Just as you use your stack of graded papers, businesses get their data from order forms, applications, payment slips, and many other documents. All these data must be organized, stored, and accessed when needed to provide information. A database management system accomplishes those important functions.

BEGINNING DATABASE FUNCTIONS

EXERCISE 4.1. HOW TO IDENTIFY FEATURES OF dBASE III PLUS

dBASE III PLUS is a relational database management system. This means that it enables you to establish several files of data and, if you wish, to relate data between files in order to answer questions and create reports.

Before getting too involved in the technical aspects of dBASE III PLUS, it is important to understand a few terms common to data management programs and used throughout this section of the guide. They are:

<u>Database.</u> A collection of related data files. For example, a business might compile a customer database.

<u>File.</u> Data related to a single subject are stored in a file. In the Customer data, one file might contain customer names and addresses while another file

might have data on what each customer has ordered.

Record. Each file contains many records. Each customer in the order file would have his/her own record.

Fields. Each record is made up of one or more fields. Within a single customer record, the fields might consist of such things as name, address, phone number, and account number.

A Look at the Structure of a Database File

So you can fully grasp what dBASE is capable of doing, look at a simple example. Refer to Figure 4-1. Section a shows data on five customers of Avalanche Outfitters, a mail-order firm.

CUSTNUM	NAME	STREET	CITY	STATE	ZIP	CHARGE
810	John T. Smith	31 Cedarcrest	Boulder	CO	80302	.T.
775	Sally Jones	725 Agua Fria	Santa Fe	NM	87501	.T.
690	William Holmes	3269 Fast Lane	Santa Fe	NM	87501	.F.
840	Artis Smith	2332 Alameda	Lakewood	CO	80215	.T.
574	Nellie Deutsch	23 E. Spruce	Olathe	KS	66061	.F.

(a) CUSTOMER file

PRODNUM	DESCRIP	PRICE
001	Nordic hat	10.00
002	Nylon windpants	40.00
003	Thermal ski socks	7.00
004	Indy Jones jacket, large	90.00
005	Rozelle headband	6.00

(b) PRODUCT file

ORDNUM	CUSTNUM	DATE
001	775	02/03/90
002	775	02/05/90
003	810	02/07/90
004	574	02/16/90
005	810	02/16/90
006	810	02/18/90

(c) ORDER file

(Continued)

(Continued)

ORDNUM	QTY	PRODNUM
001	2	003
001	1	002
002	1	001
003	1	001
003	3	003
004	1	001
004	1	003
005	2	003
006	1	004
006	1	005

(d) ODETAILS file

Figure 4-1. Database Files

Looking at Section a, identify each of the components previously discussed (database, file, record, and field) as you read through the next paragraph.

Section a of the figure shows a CUSTOMER file containing several customer records. Each record contains several fields: CUSTNUM, NAME, STREET, CITY, STATE, ZIP, and CHARGE. The first record in this file is the one on John T. Smith. The third record is on William Holmes. You might later sort this file by the field CUSTNUM in ascending order (places records in order by CUSTNUM with smallest, 574, first).

To further see how dBASE can handle database files and relate data among them, look at the database files in Figure 4-1, Sections b through d. The PRODUCT file consists of individual orders placed by customers (who are in the CUSTOMER file); the ORDER file shows when each order was placed and is sorted by the field ORDNUM; the ODETAILS file shows the product number and total quantity of each purchase and includes information from the ORDER and PRODUCT files. You should note that the files in Sections b, c, and d, respectively, contain 5, 6, and 10 records, all consisting of 3 fields. These files are drawing data from each other to form conclusions about product sales. As you can see, questions can be asked and data can be grouped together in a variety of fashions from any existing database file. The ability to draw from any number of files is the major feature of a *relational database program.*

You could also tap the CUSTOMER file for a listing of all customers from Colorado. Or, you could use that same file to prepare mailing labels for catalogs that are to be sent out next month.

On occasion, Avalanche Outfitters may want to relate data appearing in different database files. For example, if you have ever ordered anything through the mail, you have probably received an invoice similar to the one shown in Figure 4-2.

Order number: 001

Date placed: 02/03/90

Ship to: Sally Jones
725 Agua Fria
Santa Fe, NM 87501

Quantity	Description	Unit Price	Total Price
2	Thermal ski socks	$ 7.00	$ 14.00
1	Nylon windpants	40.00	40.00
			$ 54.00

Remit check to: AVALANCHE OUTFITTERS
P. O. Box 8000
Boulder, CO 80302

Figure 4-2. An Invoice Prepared from a Relational Database System (With Data from the Four Database Files in Figure 4-1)

This invoice contains data from several database files. When the order is placed, separate records are created in Avalanche's ORDER and ODETAIL files. The invoice name and shipping address are extracted from the CUSTOMER file; the prices and descriptions are extracted from the PRODUCT file; the date is taken from the ORDER file; and the quantities ordered are taken from the ODETAILS file. The computational features of the database system then produce the totals in the last column. Thus, through the power of database technology, an invoice can be prepared quickly, with minimal possibility of error.

There could be a variety of reasons you may want to relate data appearing in different database files. Avalanche's management, for example, may want the names of all customers who have ordered more than $1,000 worth of merchandise during 1990. Or, an angry customer might call claiming to have ordered a Nordic hat rather than a large Indy Jones jacket, requiring Avalanche personnel to reconstruct the original order.

Most of the examples you will see in this guide involve working on only one database file at a time. In fact, many of the data management problems you will probably face in your lifetime will be simple enough not to involve relating data between database files. Nonetheless, the ability to relate data between files is a relatively common application, and it is what database management systems are all about. An example is included later in the guide to show you how dBASE can work with multiple files. Even though you may not need to relate data yourself, you will probably encounter a lot of database management systems in various settings—from the mail-order firms that sell you clothes to the taxing agencies that use your social security number to relate files of data on your interest-bearing financial transactions. You should at least be familiar with how these systems work.

To do anything useful in dBASE, you must first learn how to define data and how to manipulate data. It's time to get started.

EXERCISE 4.2. HOW TO GET STARTED

Installing dBASE on a hard disk system:

To install dBASE on your hard disk, do the following steps. (If dBASE is already on your hard disk, skip this section.)

1. Make a new directory for dBASE. At the C> prompt, type **MD DBASE.**

2. Make this the current directory by typing **CD DBASE**

3. Load dBASE System Disk 1 into Drive A. At the C> prompt, type **COPY A:*.* C:.**

4. Load dBASE System Disk 2 into Drive A. At the C> prompt, type **COPY A:*.*C:.**

dBASE is now installed on your hard disk. To start using dBASE immediately,

5. At the C>, type **DBASE**

6. When the copyright screen appears, press **Enter**

Starting up dBASE on a hard disk system:

If your necessary dBASE disks are already stored in a file on the hard drive (C>) in a directory of their own, follow these steps each time you want to start up dBASE. (You may need to check with your instructor as to the exact name of the directory. For this exercise, it will be assumed that the directory is dBASE.)

1. Insert your formatted data disk into Drive A

2. At the C> prompt, type **cd dBASE**

3. Press **Enter**

4. From your dBASE C> prompt, type **dBASE**

5. Press **Enter**

6. At the copyright information screen, press **Enter** as instructed at the bottom of the screen

You are now in dBASE.

<u>From a dual disk system:</u>

Be sure your computer is booted with DOS and shows the system prompt, A>.

1. Insert the System 1 disk into Drive A and close the drive door

2. Put your data disk into Drive B and close the door

3. At the A>, type **dBASE**

4. Press **Enter**

5. At the copyright information screen, press **Enter** as instructed at the bottom of your screen

6. At the next screen, take the System 1 disk out of Drive A and insert the System 2 disk into Drive A. Close the door.

7. Press **Enter**

You are now in dBASE in what is called the ASSIST mode, as shown in Figure 4-3.

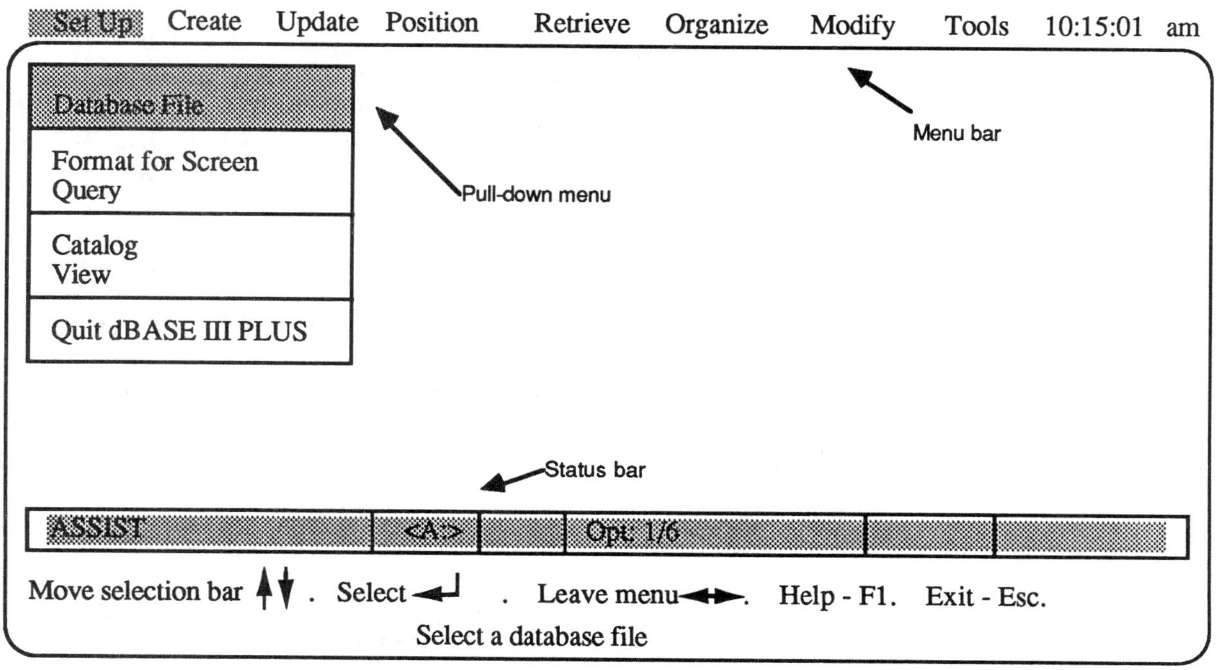

Figure 4-3. The ASSIST Mode Screen

ASSIST and COMMAND Modes

dBASE III PLUS commands can be issued in either of two modes.

The menu-driven mode uses a routine called dBASE III PLUS Assistant, or ASSIST. The ASSIST mode (or menu-driven mode) is designed to allow you to work through a sequence of steps with the assistance of menus. It consists of a system of top-of-screen menu bars and pull-down menus (the menu for "Set up" is shown in Figure 4-3) that enable commands to be issued by highlighting them with the screen cursor and then pressing the Enter key.

The interactive COMMAND mode is designed for the user who wants to issue commands as quickly as possible from the keyboard. The COMMAND mode allows you to enter command words at a dot prompt; the commands you *enter* in COMMAND mode are the same as those you *select* in ASSIST mode.

To Move through the ASSIST Mode

1. To move from menu to menu in the ASSIST mode, you use the left and right arrow keys or press the first character of each menu (much like 1-2-3 and Joe). For example, to select “Update” when “Set up” is highlighted, press the **Right Arrow** key twice or just type **U.** Practice doing this now.

2. Look at Figure 4-3. The line at the bottom of the screen is the status bar. On the first line of the status bar is stated the mode in which you are currently working: ASSIST. It also shows the current default drive, A: (or C: with a hard disk system). The third item in the status bar, Opt: 1/6, states that you are now highlighting Option 1 of 6 options available in the menu you have pulled down.

   The second line of the status bar directs you to use the up or down arrow keys to move through the selections in the menu; to press Enter to Select an item; to press the left or right arrows to Leave the menu and move to another one; to press F1 to access Help; or to press Esc to Exit the ASSIST mode.

To Move through the COMMAND Mode

1. Press the **Esc** key now

You have moved to the dot prompt. (When in ASSIST mode, press the Esc key to go to the dot prompt mode; when at the dot prompt, return to the ASSIST mode by either typing ASSIST at the dot or pressing the F2 key.)

2. Issue commands at the dot prompt

3. Press **F2** to return to the ASSIST mode

To Set the Default Drive

As with other programs, one of the first things you should do is set the default drive (to show which drive will access [save or retrieve] your data files). It is possible that your student version comes with the default already set to B:, however, it is good to know the steps for setting the default, especially if you plan to use a hard drive system.

<u>From the ASSIST mode:</u>

1. Press **T** to move to the Tools menu

2. "Set drive" will be highlighted

3. Press **Enter**

4. Press the arrow keys to highlight the drive of your choice (either A: with a hard drive or B: with a dual disk)

5. Press **Enter**

Notice that the status bar now shows your default drive.

From the COMMAND mode:

You can also set the default drive quickly from the COMMAND mode. To do so, you would first press Esc to obtain the dot prompt (.).

a. If using a dual disk system, type **SET DEFAULT TO B:** and press **Enter**
b. If using a hard disk system, type **SET DEFAULT TO A:** and press **Enter**

To Create a Database File

1. In the ASSIST mode, press **C** for Create to move to the Create menu

2. Press the arrow keys to highlight the Database file option

3. Press **Enter**

A list of drives appears on the screen. These are your options for the drive on which you want to store the new database file.

4. Highlight B: (dual-disk) or A: (hard disk)

5. Press **Enter**

6. Type **CUSTOMER** as the name of the file

7. Press **Enter**

You are now ready to identify your fields and are in the fresh database screen shown in Figure 4-4(a).

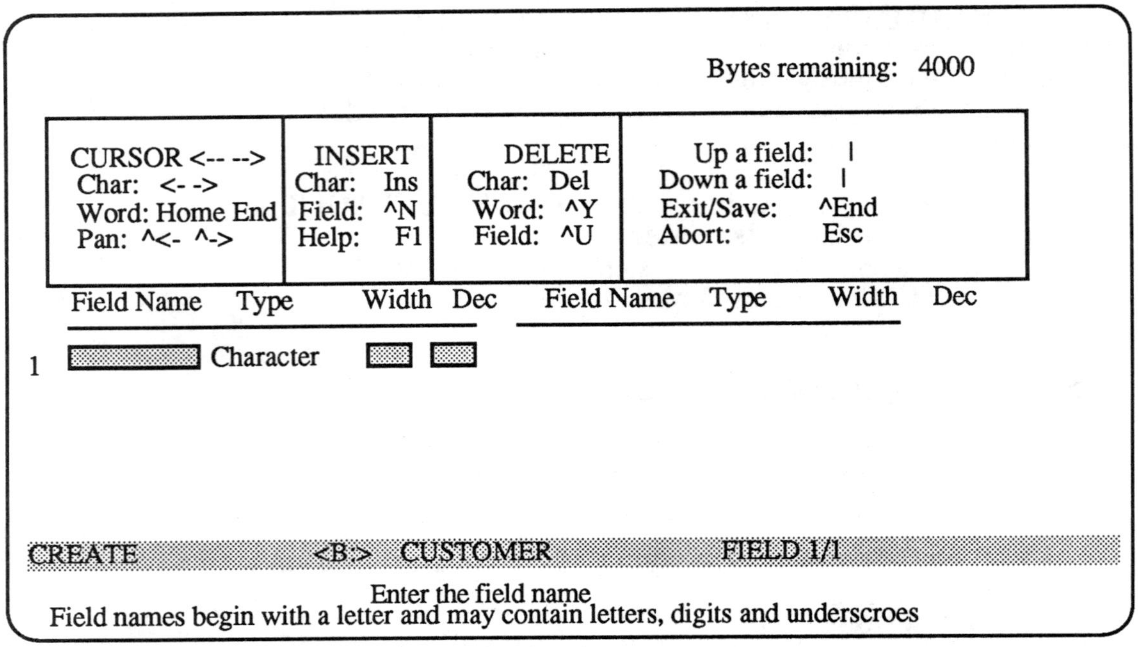

(a) Fresh Screen

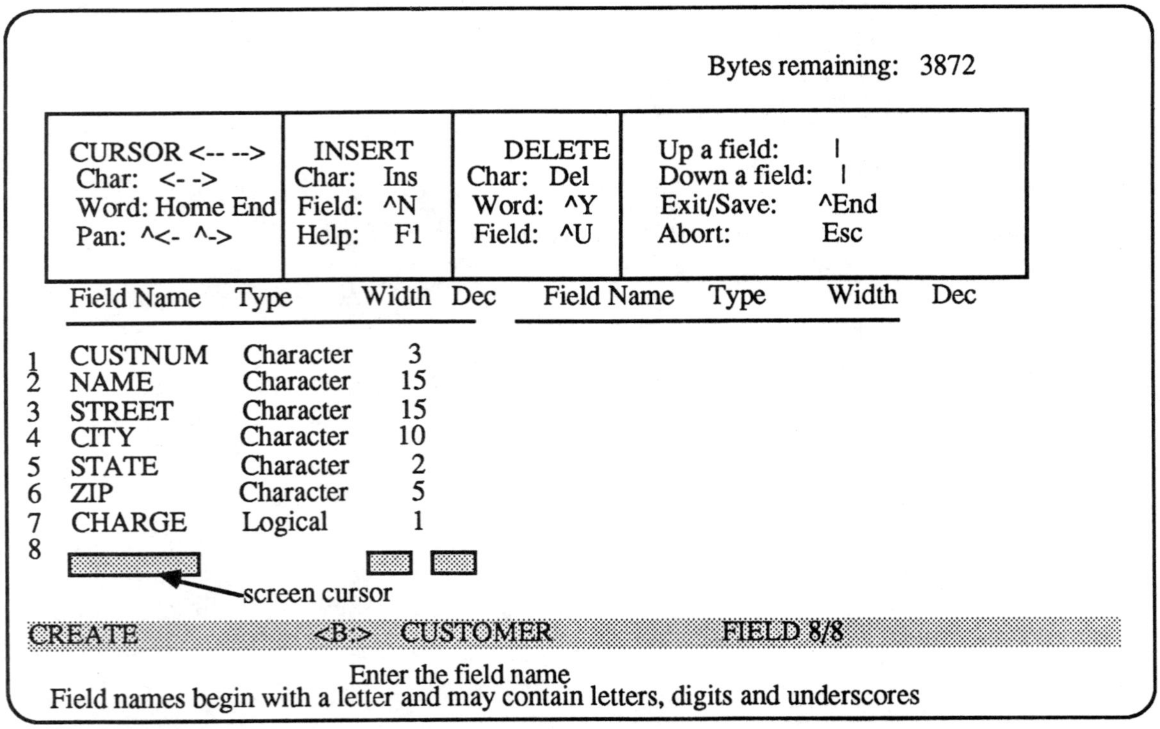

(b) Completed Screen

Figure 4-4. The Create Database Structure

In Figure 4-1 you looked at four database files. The process of describing to dBASE the physical characteristics of each of these files—how many fields they have, the names of each field, and so forth—is called *data definition*.

For example, look at the file in Figure 4-1(a). You could describe the physical characteristics, or structure, of this file as follows:

Filename: CUSTOMER

Field	Field Name	Field Type	Field Width
1	CUSTNUM	Character	3
2	NAME	Character	15
3	STREET	Character	15

You first provide dBASE with the name of the file (as you just did with CUSTOMER). Then you describe the characteristics of each field. For example, your first field name is going to be CUSTNUM. It will be described as a character field, because you do not want to perform calculations with the field, and it will be three characters wide (maximum).

The field types of the structure are called *field descriptors*. Five of these descriptors are shown in Figure 4-5.

Field Type	Maximum Data Length	Description
Character	254 characters	Character fields store data that cannot be arithmetically manipulated. You can, however, sort, index, or compare on these fields.
Numeric	19 characters	Numeric fields, which store integer numbers or numbers that contain decimal points, can be arithmetically manipulated. Numbers upon which you do not need to do arithmetic—such as employee identification numbers—should be stored in character rather than numeric fields.
Logical	1 character	Logical fields store a single character of data—a "T" (for true) or an "F" (for false), or, alternatively, a "Y" (for yes) and an "N" (for no). Tests on logical

(Continued)

(Continued)

Field Type	Maximum Data Length	Description
		fields can be used to select records from a file, as can tests on character, numeric, and date fields.
Date	8 characters	Date fields store dates, provided they are in the format MM/DD/YY (such as 12/31/87). You can sort or index on date fields, and you can also subtract them in order to calculate the number of days elapsing between two dates.
Memo	5,000 characters	Memo fields are used to store text nformation. They cannot be arithmetically manipulated or compared, but they can be edited and output, as can any other field.

Figure 4-5. Five dBASE Field Descriptors

The logical field descriptor typically carries either the value "T" or "F" (to represent True or False). In the CUSTOMER file in Figure 4-1(a), the CHARGE field uses this descriptor to distinguish charge from cash customers (T indicates a charge customer). The date field descriptor, which is present in the ORDER file of Figure 4-1(c), is used for fields that consist of dates that are stored in the format MM/DD/YY. The variable-length memo field descriptor is used for large blocks of text data, which will not require sorting, comparison, or arithmetic manipulation.

To enter the field descriptors:

1. Enter the first field, as shown in Figure 4-4(b), as follows:

   a. Type the Field Name, **CUSTNUM**
   b. Press **Enter**
   c. Press **C** for Character or **Enter** if the "type" is already Character
   d. Type **3** for the "Width" of the field
   e. Press **Enter**

2. Follow the preceding steps for entering the Field Name, Type, and Width shown for numbers 2 through 6 in Figure 4-4(b). Press **Enter** to move from field to field.

Use the up or down arrow keys to move up or down a field to make corrections in the record as you go.

3. For Field 7:

   a. Type **CHARGE** as the Field Name
   b. Press **Enter**
   c. Press **L** for Logical as the Type

The width is automatically set at 1. The response for any logical answer is always one character—either Yes or No or True or False (Y or N or T or F respectively).

You are now in the blank field, 8.

4. Press **Ctrl End** (^End) to save this file structure and Exit

5. At the message,

   ENTER to confirm?

   press **Enter**

6. At the message,

   Input data records now? (Y/N)

   press **N** for No

(This is the option that allows you to enter data after determining the structure of your file.)

The menu in Figure 4-1 (ASSIST mode) reappears. dBASE is awaiting your next command.

When you use the CREATE command to set up a database file, dBASE will allocate space on the disk for this file and record its name in your disk's directory (with a .DBF extension). Hence, the database file you have just defined has been saved as:

CUSTOMER.DBF

on your disk. You may refer to it throughout as:

CUSTOMER

After you have described the structure of a file to dBASE (as you just did with the CREATE command), you can enter records into the file and do useful things with these records. For example, at some point, you will probably want to add, delete, or modify records. You may also want a listing on your printer of certain records in a particular file. As you saw with Avalanche Outfitters, you may want to relate files to produce invoices or informative reports. Whatever the case, the process of doing anything to the fields, whose structures you have previously defined to dBASE, is called *data manipulation*.

To manipulate file data in any way, dBASE requires that you first make the file active. This is done either by pointing (having it in active memory) to it or by identifying it in some way. In dBASE, you can only point to one file at a time. When you point to a file, you can add records to it, delete records from it, modify its records, extract records from it, sort it, and do a number of other useful tasks. With some commands dBASE also lets you identify "secondary" files that you might want to join, or relate, to the file you are currently using.

The COMMAND Mode

As mentioned earlier, commands may be given from either the ASSIST mode or the COMMAND mode. Escape now to the dot prompt of the COMMAND mode.

1. Press **Esc**

Your screen is now blank except for a status bar at the bottom of the screen and the word (DEMO) and a dot (or just the dot if not using a student version) above the status bar in the lower left corner. dBASE will display this prompt whenever it is time for you, the user, to enter a command. In the exercises included in this section, you will use both the COMMAND mode and the ASSIST mode. Sometimes it is easier to give the command from the COMMAND mode. If that is the case, only the dot prompt command will be discussed.

REMEMBER, for the COMMAND mode instructions, you do not type the dot. It is there just to show you the command position next to the dot.

NOTE: If you wish, you may temporarily remove the status bar from the screen by typing

.SET STATUS OFF and pressing **Enter**

To make the status bar reappear, type:

.SET STATUS ON

The HELP Feature

Often, as you are working with dBASE, you will be confronted with a command with which you are not familiar. When this happens, in either the ASSIST mode or the COMMAND mode, press the **F1** function key while you are actively building the command on the screen but before you select it with the Enter key. Appearing on the screen will be a box with the description of the command as well as its syntax. By pressing any other key, the box will subsequently disappear, and you will return to the screen from which you requested help.

In the COMMAND mode, you can issue a HELP command to get on-screen information about a command other than the one on which you are working. For example, if you are presently using the DISPLAY command and you want information on the SORT command,

1. Type **.HELP SORT**

2. Press **Enter**

The APPEND Command

The APPEND command is used to place records in a file. This command tells dBASE that you want to add records to the end of a file. If there are no records in the file, the APPEND command automatically points you to the first record position. On the other hand, if there are already 15 records in the file, APPEND will point to the 16th record position.

In the COMMAND mode:

1. Type **.APPEND** (in upper or lower case)

2. Press **Enter**

or

In the ASSIST mode:

1. Choose Append from the Update menu

This command allows you to add records to the CUSTOMER file after it has been opened or just after it has been created (as you just did). Once you issue this command, you will be given a screen similar to the one in Figure 4-6.

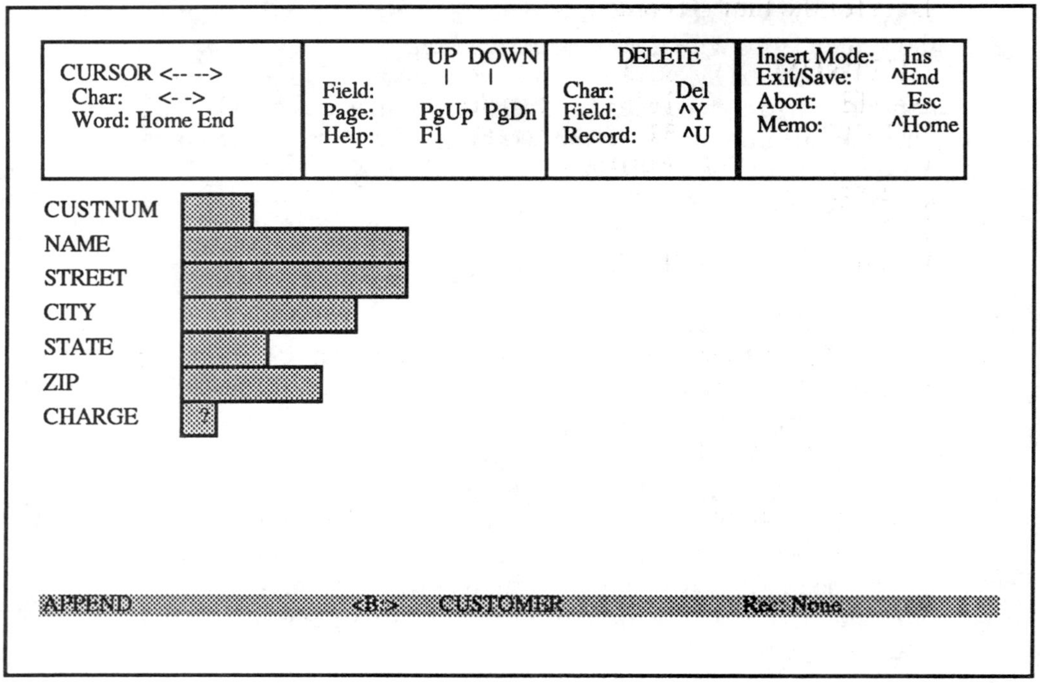

Figure 4-6. The APPEND Screen

NOTE: This template has a reverse-video, highlighted data area sized consistently with the structure you described when first creating the fields (e.g., setting the width). Since, at this point, you have not entered any records into the CUSTOMER file, do the following:

2. Type the data for the first record as shown below using the following guidelines:
   a. When the data fills up the entire shaded area, you do not need to press Enter; the cursor will automatically move to the next line and a "beep" will sound
   b. When the data does not fill up the shaded area, press **Enter** to continue
   c. Look at the menus at the top of the screen to note the movement from field to field and for such commands as saving
   d. When you reach the last field, and enter "T" in the CHARGE field, a new blank record will be presented so you can continue filling in the data for the next record

Data for the First Record:

CUSTNUM	**810**
NAME	**John T. Smith**
STREET	**31 Cedarcrest**
CITY	**Boulder**
STATE	**CO**
ZIP	**80302**
CHARGE	**T**

In the fourth area of your status bar at the bottom of the screen is the message:

Rec:EOF/1

indicating that one record is in the file and that dBASE is pointing to the end of the file.

3. Add the following records:

775
Sally Jones
725 Agua Fria
Santa Fe
NM
87501
T

690
William Holmes
3269 Fast Lane
Santa Fe
NM
87501
F

840
Artis Smith
2332 Alameda
Lakewood
CO
80215
T

574
Nellie Deutsch
23 E. Spruce
Olathe
KS
66061
F

When you have entered all of the records (and the next blank record is showing),

4. Press **Ctrl End** (hold the Ctrl key down while you press the End key)

To List Records in a File

<u>In the COMMAND mode:</u>

1. Type **.LIST**

at the dot prompt

2. Press **Enter**

or

<u>In the ASSIST mode:</u>

1. Choose List from the Retrieve menu

2. Choose the Execute the command option from the submenu that appears

3. Press **N** to the prompt,

   Direct the output to the printer? [Y/N]

This will produce a listing like the one shown in Figure 4-7.

Record#	CUSTNUM	NAME	STREET	CITY	STATE	ZIP	CHARGE
1	810	John T. Smith	31 Cedarcrest	Boulder	CO	80302	.T.
2	775	Sally Jones	725 Agua Fria	Santa Fe	NM	87501	.T.
3	690	William Holmes	3269 Fast Lane	Santa Fe	NM	87501	.F.
4	840	Artis Smith	2332 Alameda	Lakewood	CO	80215	.T.
5	574	Nellie Deutsch	23 E. Spruce	Olathe	KS	66061	.F.

Figure 4-7. Listed Output from the CUSTOMER File

To Halt a List

Sometimes listing the file gets long and cumbersome. This happens when a file contains many records, which cannot all be shown on the screen at one time. To temporarily halt the scrolling of all records, so that you can view a portion of the file at a time, you can type

Ctrl S

To begin the scrolling of the files again, type

Ctrl Q

The DISPLAY command, however (covered shortly), avoids the necessity of the Ctrl/S and Ctrl/Q sequence by allowing you to view a selected number of records at a time.

To QUIT the Database

Using the QUIT command when leaving the database closes (and thus saves) any files that might still be open. It is important to always use the QUIT command so that records added to files are not lost when you shut off the system.

In COMMAND mode:

1. Type **QUIT**

2. Press **Enter**

or

In the ASSIST mode:

1. Choose Quit dBASE III PLUS from the Set Up menu

2. Press **Enter**

Quit now and complete the review questions.

Review Questions on Exercises 4.1 and 4.2

1. Identify the hierarchy of the following database elements: record, file, fields, and database, beginning with the largest and ending with the smallest feature.

2. What is the command entered at the system prompt to start dBASE III Plus?

3. What is the first screen you see after signing onto dBASE? What can you do from this screen?

4. How are menus reached in the ASSIST mode?

5. How is the default drive set from the COMMAND mode?

6. How do you create a file from the ASSIST mode?

7. What are the field types discussed in this exercise that may be used when setting up fields in a database?

8. What is the command used to save and exit a CREATE screen or an APPEND screen?

9. What happens when you type **APPEND** in COMMAND mode?

10. What command is typed at the dot prompt (COMMAND mode) to see a display of all records entered in a file?

Answers to the Review Questions on Exercises 4.1 and 4.2

1. database, file, record, and field
2. Type **dBASE** and press **Enter**
3. The ASSIST menus. You can make selections from the menus to set the default drive, append records, create a new database, etc.
4. Using the left and right arrow keys or the first character of the menu
5. Type **.SET DEFAULT TO B:** with a dual-disk system (or **A:** with a hard disk)
6. a. Select Create menu
   b. Move to the Database option
   c. Select the default drive
   d. Name the file
7. Numeric, character, memo, logical, date
8. Ctrl End
9. You move to the first blank record in the file and may then enter data into the record
10. .LIST

EXERCISE 4.3. HOW TO EDIT A DATABASE FILE

First, sign on to the program again.

1. At the system prompt (the dBASE prompt if using a hard disk system), type **dBASE**

NOTE: It is not necessary to type capitals each time. Upper- or lowercase letters will both be recognized.

2. Press **Enter**

3. Follow the screen messages for inserting the System 2 disk if using a dual-disk system

You are now at the ASSIST menus again.

4. Press **Esc** to go to the command mode

5. Set the default drive once as you sign on, by typing **.SET DEFAULT TO B:** (or **A**: for a hard drive system)

To View Existing Files

Before opening an existing database file, such as the CUSTOMER file, it is often helpful to see all of the files on the data disk in (Drive B or A). It is easy to forget what files are stored on the disk or to forget exactly what name was given to the file.

<u>From the COMMAND mode:</u>

1. Type **.DIR**

2. Press **Enter**

A list of all .DBF files is shown. One of the files (perhaps your only file at this time) is your CUSTOMER file. Other information given with this command is the number of records in each database file and the date of the last revision. The size of the file is also displayed. This command may be used to be certain that your database file has been saved and that there are a certain number of records in the file.

From the ASSIST mode:

The ASSIST mode is useful for viewing files when you would like to see all files on your data disk and not just the .DBF files.

You just created a file with the .DBF extension. As was mentioned earlier, the .DBF extension is automatically inserted by dBASE for any file that is generated through the CREATE command. As you begin to create other kinds of files, such as indexes and reports (discussed later), dBASE will insert other extensions for those.

Some of the extensions you might see in your directory are shown in Figure 4-8.

The .DBF extension	Contains records that are composed of fields of data. The data files may be anything relating to information about business transactions or records of statistics to keep for study.
The .DBT extension	Contains memo files and contains large blocks of information found in the memo fields of database files. The information you type into any memo field is stored in this separate file.
The .NDX extension	Contains files created with the Index command. These fields provide dBASE with the ability to arrange information in a file.
The .FMT extension	Contains files that are custom screen or report forms
The .FRM extension	Contains files that have been created from creating a report form
The .QRY extension	Contains information about conditions for displaying records from an existing database file
The .SCR extension	Contains files with information about the screen layout for custom data entry forms

(Continued)

(Continued)

In addition to these extensions, you might also see one of the following:

.MEM	A memory file
.VUE	A view file
.LBL	A label file

Figure 4-8. File Extensions Shown from the Tools Menu

1. Press **F2** to return to the ASSIST mode

   or

   Type **ASSIST** at the dot prompt

2. Press **T** to move to the Tools menu
3. Highlight Directory
4. Press **Enter**
5. Press **Enter** on the B: (dual-disk) or A: (hard disk)

A list of file extensions appears. Notice that there are several extensions, including those mentioned in Figure 4-8.

6. Highlight the .DBF file extensions
7. Press **Enter**

A list of your database files appears. The CUSTOMER file is shown with the number of bytes used.

8. Press **Esc** twice until you reach the dot prompt

To Open the Customer File

Now that you know what files are contained on your disk, you can open one of them.

1. In COMMAND mode (dot prompt), type
   .USE CUSTOMER
2. Press **Enter**

The CUSTOMER filename is now showing in the status bar, which means that it is the active, or open, file.

To DELETE Records

Deleting a record permanently from a dBASE file requires two steps:

a. The DELETE command is issued to "flag" the record to be deleted. At this point, the record will be preceded by an asterisk (*) indicating it has been identified as one to be deleted, but it is still actively part of the file. You can restore the record, if you wish, by issuing a RECALL command.
b. The PACK command is issued to permanently delete the record. The PACK command causes dBASE to drop all records with delete (*) flags from the file. After the file has been packed, the deleted records no longer exist and cannot be recalled.

In the COMMAND mode:

The easiest way to mark records for deletion, permanently delete them, or recall them is from the COMMAND mode (dot prompt).

1. Type **.DELETE RECORD 5**

2. Press **Enter**

The message "1 record deleted" appears on your screen.

3. Type **.LIST**

Notice that Record 5 has an asterisk next to it. It is marked for deletion, but is not yet permanently deleted, so you have the option of changing your mind.

To recall a record marked for deletion:

You can recall a record that has been marked for deletion, so that it is no longer marked. Do this for Record 5. Again, the easiest method for recalling a record is from the COMMAND mode, so only this method will be discussed.

1. Type **.RECALL RECORD 5**

2. Press **Enter**

The message "1 record recalled" appears on your screen.

3. List the file again to confirm that the asterisk is gone

Figure 4-9(a) shows what your screen will look like when you delete and then recall a record.

To Apply the PACK Command

If, instead of recalling a record, you wanted to follow through with the deletion, you would apply the PACK command. This command permanently deletes the marked file. In your file, you have an extra blank record, 6. It was added automatically when you were appending your database file, because your last field (CHARGE) was exactly the width of your data entry (.T. or .F.), so you were automatically moved to the next blank record. To eliminate the empty record permanently,

1. Mark Record 6 for deletion by typing
   .DELETE RECORD 6
2. List the file to be sure the record is marked
3. Type **.PACK**
4. Press **Enter**

The message "5 records copied" appears.

5. List the file again to confirm that the record is deleted

The record is deleted, and the remaining records are automatically renumbered sequentially. This process is visually presented in Figure 4-9(b).

```
.DELETE RECORD 5 (Enter)
      (1 record deleted)
.LIST (Enter)
Record  CUSTNUM  NAME              STREET           CITY       STATE  ZIP    CHARGE
1         810    John T. Smith     31 Cedarcrest    Boulder    CO     80302   .T.
2         775    Sally Jones       725 Agua Fria    Santa Fe   NM     87501   .T.
3         690    William Holmes    3269 Fast Lane   Santa Fe   NM     87501   .F.
4         840    Artis Smith       2332 Alameda     Lakewood   CO     80215   .T.
5         574    Nellie Deutsch    23 E. Spruce     Olathe     KS     66061   .F.
.RECALL RECORD 5 (Enter)
 1 record recalled
.LIST (Enter)
Record  CUSTNUM  NAME              STREET           CITY       STATE  ZIP    CHARGE
1         810    John T. Smith     31 Cedarcrest    Boulder    CO     80302   .T.
2         775    Sally Jones       725 Agua Fria    Santa Fe   NM     87501   .T.
3         690    William Holmes    3269 Fast Lane   Santa Fe   NM     87501   .F.
4         840    Artis Smith       2332 Alameda     Lakewood   CO     80215   .T.
5         574    Nellie Deutsch    23 E. Spruce     Olathe     KS     66061   .F.
```

(a) Deleting a record and later recalling it

```
.DELETE RECORD 6 (Enter)
      1 record deleted
.LIST (Enter)
Record  CUSTNUM  NAME             STREET          CITY        STATE  ZIP     CHARGE
1       810      John T. Smith    31 Cedarcrest   Boulder     CO     80302   .T.
2       775      Sally Jones      725 Agua Fria   Santa Fe    NM     87501   .T.
3       690      William Holmes   3269 Fast Lane  Santa Fe    NM     87501   .F.
4       840      Artis Smith      2332 Alameda    Lakewood    CO     80215   .T.
5       574      Nellie Deutsch   23 E. Spruce    Olathe      KS     66061   .F.
6         *
.PACK (Enter)
 5 records copied
.LIST (Enter)
Record  CUSTNUM  NAME             STREET          CITY        STATE  ZIP     CHARGE
1       810      John T. Smith    31 Cedarcrest   Boulder     CO     80302   .T.
2       775      Sally Jones      725 Agua Fria   Santa Fe    NM     87501   .T.
3       690      William Holmes   3269 Fast Lane  Santa Fe    NM     87501   .F.
4       840      Artis Smith      2332 Alameda    Lakewood    CO     80215   .T.
5       574      Nellie Deutsch   23 E. Spruce    Olathe      KS     66061   .F.
```

(b) Deleting a record permanently

Figure 4-9. Deleting a Record

To Change Contents of Records

Changing data in records may be necessary for a variety of reasons. A customer may have moved, requiring a street address to be changed. The price of a product may have gone up. Data originally typed into a field may have been incorrect. Whatever the case, editing allows you to change the values contained in the fields of any database records. You can edit records either one at a time, by using the EDIT command, or you can display several records on-screen at the same time and edit them with the BROWSE command.

To Use BROWSE

One of the fastest ways to edit your records is through the use of the BROWSE command. You have the option of selecting Browse from the Update menu in the ASSIST mode or entering Browse through the COMMAND mode.

<u>From the ASSIST mode:</u>

1. Type **U** to select the Update menu

2. Select Browse

3. Press **Enter**

From the dot prompt in the COMMAND mode:

1. Type **.BROWSE**

2. Press **Enter**

Once you're in Browse,

1. Press **Pg Up** once to see all of your records at one time

2. Use arrow keys to move from record to record or from field to field. As soon as you see data that need to be updated, type in the updates over the original data.

   In your CUSTOMER file, make the following corrections:

   a. Sally Jones's customer number is actually 778
   b. The charge field for William Holmes should read .T.

If you had a very large database file and were using the BROWSE command to edit it, you could press the F1 key to have the boxed menu at the top of the screen disappear.

The PgUp and PgDn keys also allow you to scroll through records a screenful at a time.

Sometimes records are too long to fit on a Browse screen. When this happens, press the **Ctrl** key and also the **Right Arrow** key to pan to fields currently located off-screen. Use the Ctrl/Left Arrow key combination to pan in the other direction.

3. When you have finished making editing corrections, press **Ctrl End**

Both Ctrl End and Ctrl W tell dBASE that you are finished with the edit and want to save the changes. Also, those keystroke combinations will return you to the COMMAND (dot prompt) mode.

NOTE: You could also press the Esc key if you decided not to save the changes made in the Browse mode. But be careful about using the Esc key for this purpose, because you will lose all changes you made in Browse.

To Use EDIT

You can edit in the COMMAND mode (at the dot prompt) through the use of the ASSIST menus.

In ASSIST mode:

1. Type **U** to select the Update menu

2. Select the Edit option

3. Press **Enter**

In the COMMAND mode (dot prompt):

1. Type **.EDIT**

2. Press **Enter**

You can use a number of editing features available in dBASE III PLUS to make changes in a record. The options available to you are shown in Figure 4-10.

Cursor Control Key	OR	dBASE Command	Action
		CTRL/A	Moves the cursor one word to the left
		CTRL/F	Moves the cursor one word to the right
←		CTRL/S	Moves the cursor one position to the left
→		CTRL/D	Moves the cursor one position to the right
↑		CTRL/E	Moves the cursor up one line. At the top of the line it displays the prior record.
↓		CTRL/X	Moves the cursor down one line. At the bottom line it displays the next record.
Del		CTRL/G	Deletes the character at the cursor position and moves the text one position to the left
		CTRL/Y	Deletes the contents of an entire field.
		CTRL/W	Writes the changes back to the file. It then returns you to the ASSIST menu.
PgUp		CTRL/R	Writes the current record to disk and displays the previous record
PgDn		CTRL/C	Writes the current record to disk and displays the next record
Ins		CTRL/V	Toggles between overwrite and insert modes. In INS mode the insert message is displayed in the status bar.
		CTRL/U	Deletes or undeletes a record

Figure 4-10. Cursor Movements While in EDIT Mode

Once you're in EDIT, you can change Record 2 as follows.

1. Press **PgUp** to go to Record 2 for Jones
2. Change the street address by typing **813 Pine Bluff** over the old address
3. Press **Ctrl End** when finished

To EDIT Specific Records

You can also use the EDIT command to edit specific types of records. For example, you might want to edit all Colorado records. Again, this type of command is done more easily through the COMMAND (dot) mode.

In COMMAND mode:

1. Type **.EDIT FOR STATE = 'CO'**

2. Press **Enter**

All Colorado records (two of them) are retrieved for editing. You can move from record to record with the PgDn and PgUp keys. The John T. Smith record is now showing.

3. Change the CUSTNUM for them as follows:

   Smith, John T. to 820
   Smith, Artis to 850

4. Press **Ctrl End** when finished

This EDIT command used a conditional expression, STATE = 'CO', to search for specific records.

5. Use the LIST command to see that the record has been properly changed

To Add Records to the Database

You add records in the same way that you first entered information in this exercise, with the use of the APPEND command. When first entering the data into the fields in your CUSTOMER file, you used the APPEND command from the Update menu (unless you are an experienced user and jumped ahead to the dot prompt).

Now that you have been using the COMMAND mode frequently, you can practice appending records in the same manner.

1. Type **.APPEND** at the dot prompt

2. Press **Enter**

You are now ready to add records to the current file. Notice that the status line tells you that you are at the end of your file (EOF) on the last record. Remember that you will be adding records to the database file that is active. And the last active file was the CUSTOMER file. The active file is showing in the third box of the status panel at the bottom of the screen. If you had opened other files while working with dBASE, the APPEND command would be in effect for the most recently opened file.

3. Enter the following data into new records in your CUSTOMER file. As you reach the end of each record, a new record will automatically appear.

Record#	CUSTNUM	NAME	STREET	CITY	STATE	ZIP	CHARGE
6	447	Vernon Pressy	5541 Canyon	Boulder	CO	80302	.T.
7	480	Benton Fink	440 Arapahoe	Boulder	CO	80302	.F.
8	401	Wayne Montoya	600 Tara Lane	Englewood	CO	80155	.F.
9	640	C. Foster Kane	P.O. Box 6000	Santa Fe	NM	87501	.T.
10	505	Alice Evans	5702 North St.	Boise	ID	83704	.T.
11	102	Maya Ellis	603 Oakwood	Aurora	CO	80011	.T.
12	754	Shane Williams	275 East Kiowa	Flagstaff	AZ	86001	.F.
13	801	Del Lopez	80 Williston	Austin	TX	78755	.F.
14	908	Duke Miller	CM Ranch	Stanley	NM	87056	.F.
15	665	Bette White	Box 20	Rowe	NM	87562	.T.
16	760	Kim Lundy	44West St.	Missoula	MT	59802	.F.
17							

4. Press **Ctrl End** when finished

5. List the file to proof it

6. Append any records if necessary, or Browse or Edit the records until they are correct

7. Delete and Pack Record 17

8. Quit or continue to the next lesson

Review Questions for Exercise 4.3

All questions in this review will refer to commands entered from the COMMAND mode (dot prompt) unless otherwise stated.

1. List the steps necessary to set the default drive.

2. What command is used to view all .DBF files on a disk?

3. What steps are used to view all files (.DBF and otherwise) when in the ASSIST mode?

4. How are records marked for deletion?

5. How are records permanently deleted?

6. What command is used to edit and scroll through all records at once?

7. What command is generally used to make corrections on a specific record?

8. What command is used to add records to a database file?

Answers to the Review Questions on Exercise 4.3

1. .SET DEFAULT TO B: (dual disk) A: (hard disk)
2. .DIR
3. T for the Tools menu, Directory, B: or A:, .DBF or another extension, Enter
4. .DELETE RECORD 8 (or any other record number)
5. .PACK
6. .BROWSE
7. .EDIT RECORD 8 (or any other record)
8. .APPEND

INTERMEDIATE DATABASE FUNCTIONS

EXERCISE 4.4. HOW TO MANIPULATE dBASE

Up to this point, everything you have done in dBASE has involved learning how to create and maintain files. Now it is time to use dBASE as a tool for extracting valuable information from a file.

To show how this can be done, you will use the enlarged CUSTOMER file created in the last lesson.

1. Open the CUSTOMER file through the COMMAND mode (if necessary)

   Type **.USE CUSTOMER**

2. Press **Enter**

The CUSTOMER file is active.

There are many ways to extract data from dBASE files.

3. List the CUSTOMER file to make sure all records are present and correct (16 of them)

To Display Records in the COMMAND Mode

Below are three rather different examples of extracting data with the DISPLAY command. The third example, on relational operators, will lead to five other examples using relational symbols and connectors.

<u>The .DISPLAY ALL OFF command:</u>

1. Type **.DISPLAY ALL OFF**
2. Press **Enter**

This statement is similar (but not identical) to the LIST command. The keyword ALL causes all records to be displayed on the screen. The keyword OFF suppresses the record numbers. A major difference between Display and List is that Display causes records to be displayed a screen at a time, whereas List causes them to be scrolled onto (and possibly off of) the screen. For long files (with Display), you can press any key to get the next screen of records.

The .DISPLAY ALL OFF CUSTNUM, NAME, CHARGE command:

1. Type **.DISPLAY ALL OFF CUSTNUM, NAME, CHARGE**

2. Press **Enter**

This form of the DISPLAY command identifies specific fields to be displayed. Thus, only the CUSTNUM, NAME, and CHARGE fields of your CUSTOMER file are output.

The .DISPLAY ALL OFF FOR STATE = "CO" command:

1. Type **.DISPLAY ALL OFF FOR STATE = "CO"**

2. Press **Enter**

This statement produces a listing of all records with "CO" (Colorado) as the STATE field. The FOR clause, when used with the DISPLAY command, tells dBASE to select only those records meeting the conditional expression that follows the keyword FOR.

Conditional expressions:

Conditional expressions in dBASE are constructed much the same way as in some programming languages, such as BASIC, Pascal, COBOL, and FORTRAN. That is, they are typically formed by a field name, followed by one or more relational operators (such as = or >) and a constant. For example,

STATE = "NM" (equal to)
CITY = "Boulder"
ZIP = "80302"
CUSTNUM <= "505" (less than or equal to)

NOTE: The character constants (such as "NM," "Boulder," and "ZIP") appear in quotes. Also be aware that, regarding literal expressions within quotes, dBASE distinguishes upper- from lowercase characters so that if NM is in uppercase, be sure to use uppercase in the expression. Numeric fields do not need to be in quotes.

<u>And, Or, and Not expressions:</u>

Compound expressions can be formed using one or more of the three connectors:

.NOT.
.AND.
.OR.

If you want a listing of all records representing states other than Colorado

1. Type **.DISPLAY ALL OFF FOR .NOT. STATE = "CO"**

2. Press **Enter**

All states other than Colorado are listed.

Or, if you want a listing of records representing customers from either New Mexico or Colorado

1. Type **.DISPLAY ALL OFF FOR STATE = "NM" .OR. STATE = "CO"**

2. Press **Enter**

All New Mexico and Colorado records are listed.

The .OR. connector causes selection of records meeting either or both conditions. In this particular case, the way the file is set up, it is actually impossible for a person to be both from Colorado and from New Mexico, however, you could do the following

1. Type **.DISPLAY ALL OFF FOR STATE = "NM" .OR. CHARGE**

2. Press **Enter**

With this statement it is possible to find customers who meet one or both conditions—that is,

* They are from New Mexico, but they don't have a charge account
* They are not from New Mexico, but they have a charge account
* They are from New Mexico, and they have a charge account

The use of the logical field name, CHARGE, implies the logical relation CHARGE = ".T." This type of construction is used for logical field comparisons only.

The .AND. connector is used to display only records meeting both of the conditions that it joins. For example,

1. Type **.DISPLAY ALL OFF FOR STATE = "NM" .AND. CHARGE**

2. Press **Enter**

You now see only New Mexico customers with charge accounts.

There are many other forms of the DISPLAY command and forms of conditional expressions in addition to those shown here. Unfortunately, a full discussion of these is beyond the scope of this guide. Before you go on, you might be interested in knowing that conditional expressions can be used with other dBASE commands, such as Delete and List. For example,

.DELETE FOR STATE = "CO"

would mark all Colorado records for deletion.

To Display Records in the ASSIST Mode

ASSIST uses a system of menus to construct the eight DISPLAY commands you just learned. Practice running through the following steps so that you can see how ASSIST is used and how it compares to using the COMMAND mode.

Return to the ASSIST mode by pressing **F2** or typing **.ASSIST**

1. Choose Display from the Retrieve menu

At this time you see a five-option submenu. The five options and the submenu choices they lead to are:

Execute the command:	You select this option to execute the finished DISPLAY command. You cannot effectively issue this command until you have at least specified a scope for the Display (discussed next).

Specify scope:	When you select this option you are asked to make one of five choices: Default scope, ALL, NEXT, RECORD, and REST. The most useful of these is ALL, which tells dBASE to consider all of the records in the file. If you are curious about the other options, invoke dBASE's Help feature to learn about them.
Construct a field list:	This option allows you to identify the field you want displayed. When you select this option, the field names are displayed in a submenu. You select the ones you want with the Enter key and bypass the ones you don't want by passing through them with the Down Arrow key. It is not necessary to exercise this option if you want all fields displayed.
Build a search condition:	This option allows you to specify relational operators and connectors such as AND, OR, and NOT. Using this option with menus can be tricky. Immediately above the status bar, dBASE will show the construction of the DISPLAY command suggested by your selections, to help prevent confusion.
Build a scope condition:	This option allows you to display records while a condition is true. As soon as the condition is not met, records will cease to be displayed. Again, look at the construction above the status bar to avoid confusion.

This five-choice submenu is also available with many other dBASE commands, including Delete, Recall, Edit, List, Count, Sum, and Average.

NOTE: Press **Enter** after each selection.

2. Choose Specify scope from the submenu

3. Choose ALL from the next submenu

4. Choose Execute the command option from the Display submenu

dBASE will automatically pause after 16 or 17 lines of the file are displayed on the screen. To display the next screen and subsequent files, press any key. You can continue this until you reach the end of the file you are viewing.

5. Press any key to continue.

To Display All with Specific Fields

You may want to display all records, but only specific fields of each. You can do this through the menus as well as from the dot prompt.

Remember that when you were in the COMMAND mode, you entered a command that read, DISPLAY ALL OFF CUSTNUM, NAME, CHARGE. You could issue this same command from the ASSIST mode.

1. Choose Display from the Retrieve menu

2. Choose Specify scope from the submenu

3. Choose ALL from the next submenu

4. Choose Construct a field list from the Display submenu

5. Use the arrow keys to highlight CUSTNUM and press **Enter**; you are now on Name, press **Enter**; select Charge and press **Enter**

NOTE: The command sequence appears at the bottom of your screen.

6. Press the **Right Arrow** to move to the Display submenu

7. Choose Execute the command from the Display submenu

   A list of CUSTNUM, NAME, and CHARGE appears.

8. Press any key

To Perform Calculations

Three commands that are useful for performing arithmetic on dBASE records or fields are Count, Sum, and Average. Here, you will learn how to use these commands in the COMMAND mode. All three commands are also available in ASSIST, through the Retrieve command on the menu bar.

Count

Count is used for tallying records.

1. Be sure you are in the COMMAND mode. If you are not, press **Esc** to exit to the dot prompt.

2. Be sure the CUSTOMER file is active. If it is not, type **USE CUSTOMER** and press **Enter.**

3. Type **.COUNT**

4. Press **Enter**

The result of this command is that the records are tallied. A message appears that says

> 16 records (this includes any blank records from the delete)

5. Type **.COUNT FOR STATE = "CO"**

6. Press **Enter**

The result of this command is

> 6 records

These are examples of ways to count the records for specific fields or an entire file.

Sum

In this exercise, you will create the database file shown next and perform SUM and AVERAGE commands on specified fields.

1. At the dot prompt in COMMAND mode, type **.CREATE SALES**

2. Define fields as follows:

Field name	Field type	Width	Decimal places
SUPPLIER	Character	4	
DESCRIP	Character	25	
QUANTITY	Numeric	3	0
PRICE	Numeric	6	2

3. Press **^End** (Ctrl End) when finished creating the fields; press **Enter**, and answer **Y** to input data records

4. Fill in the data as shown below. When typing the number, type 90.00 just as shown below, without pressing the spacebar to move over to the period. (The decimal place will "catch" as soon as you press period when typing the number.)

SUPPLIER	DESCRIP	QUANTITY	PRICE
Funk	Indy Jones Jacket, large	30	90.00
Funk	Rozelle Headbands	10	6.00
Peak	Nordic Hats	85	10.00
Peak	Nylon Windpants	50	40.00
Peak	Thermal Ski Socks	100	7.00

5. Press **^End** (Ctrl End) when finished

Be sure you are in COMMAND mode; press **Esc** if you are not.

Sum is used for summing fields from the records of a file. For example, the file SALES is now active, at the dot prompt

1. Type **.SUM PRICE**

2. Press **Enter**

which produces the sum 153.00.

As with the COUNT statement, you can also use a FOR clause that contains a conditional statement. For example, each product in the file has a supplier field (Funk Clothing and Peak Mountaineering). Use a statement such as:

1. **.SUM PRICE FOR SUPPLIER = "Peak"**

2. Press **Enter**

to produce the sum 57.00.

Average

Average is used for averaging a field in the records of a file. For example, the fields in the file SALES could be averaged.

1. Type **.AVERAGE PRICE**

2. Press **Enter**

to produce the average of 25.50.

Quit or continue to the next exercise.

EXERCISE 4.5. HOW TO APPLY OTHER USEFUL COMMANDS

To Index

You may want to rearrange the order of records according to a key field. Assume that you want a listing of the CUSTOMER file, in ascending order by customer number. In that case, CUSTNUM would be your key field. First you create an index file to determine the order in which CUSTOMER's records would appear if CUSTOMER were to be sorted by the CUSTNUM field. Remember that the CUSTOMER file will not change since you are creating a new output file.

The index file that you will ask dBASE to create for CUSTOMER will look approximately like the file in Figure 4-11.

Indexing Order	Record #	CUSTNUM
1	11	102
2	8	401
3	6	447
4	7	480
5	10	505
6	5	574
7	9	640
8	155	665
9	3	690
10	12	754
11	16	760
12	2	775
13	13	801
14	1	820
15	4	850
16	14	908

Figure 4-11. An Index File for the CUSTOMER File. The Key Field, CUSTNUM, Is Arranged Low to High.

NOTE: If you output the records of CUSTOMER in the order suggested by this index file (Customer 102, Customer 401, and so on) the records will be in the proper sorted sequence by CUSTNUM.

At the dot prompt in COMMAND mode and with the CUSTOMER file (.USE CUSTOMER) active,

1. Type **.INDEX ON CUSTNUM TO NUMINDX**

2. Press **Enter**

This command creates, on the default drive, an index file for CUSTOMER called NUMINDX.NDX, and the message "100% indexed" appears.

All index files stored by dBASE have the extension .NDX. This extension, as mentioned earlier and as true with all dBASE extensions, is not typed and does not need to be entered by you, the user. The index file is not a duplicate of the .DBF file; the index file contains fewer fields.

This particular index file is keyed into CUSTOMER's CUSTNUM field. To look at the sorted listing of the records in CUSTOMER,

3. Type **.SET INDEX TO NUMINDX**

4. Press **Enter**

This command told dBASE to open the NUMINDX index file. Just as .DBF files must be opened with the USE command, .NDX files are not usable unless they are first opened.

5. To list the records in sorted order, type **.LIST**

6. Press **Enter**

The customer numbers are now shown in ascending order.

Two similar sequences of operator instructions and dBASE actions are listed below. Try each of these sequences. The first will produce a list of customers by zip in ascending order. The second sequence will produce a list where the customer numbers are in order within each zip code.

To list customer zip codes in order, type the following commands:

1. **.USE CUSTOMER**

2. **.INDEX ON ZIP TO ZIPINDEX**

3. **.SET INDEX TO ZIPINDX**

4. **.LIST**

To list customer numbers in order within each zip code, type the following commands:

1. **.USE CUSTOMER**

2. **.INDEX ON ZIP +CUSTNUM TO DBLINDX**

3. **.SET INDEX TO DBLINDX**

4. **.LIST**

You can create several index files for any file with a .DBF extension.

To Apply a SORT

dBASE has a SORT command that, although conceptually more straightforward than indexing, is far less computationally efficient. Using SORT creates a new DBF file, unlike using INDEX, and thus uses much more memory.

One advantage that sorting has over indexing, however, is that it is much easier to use when files must be arranged in descending order. For example, arranging CUSTOMER in descending order by CUSTNUM is relatively easy.

At the dot prompt in COMMAND mode,

1. Type **.USE CUSTOMER** (if necessary)

2. Press **Enter**

3. Type **.SORT ON CUSTNUM/D TO NEWFILE**

NOTE: The /D tells the program to sort in descending order.

4. Press **Enter**

The first command you issued points to the file you want to sort, CUSTOMER. The second command physically sorts the file in descending order and places the results in NEWFILE. Thus, two versions of CUSTOMER now exist—an unsorted version (CUSTOMER) and a sorted version (NEWFILE). This can consume a lot of space, but, since sorting is easier than indexing, it can save time for the dBASE user.

To view the version with customer numbers sorted in descending order,

5. Type **.USE NEWFILE**

6. Type **.LIST**

As with indexing, one can sort a file on more than one field. For example, if you wanted to sort on CITY as the primary key field, sorted in ascending order, and CUSTNUM as the secondary key field, sorted in descending order, you would type the SORT command as follows:

.SORT ON CITY, CUSTNUM/D TO NEWFILE2

NOTE: Remember to have the main database file (CUSTOMER) open each time the SORT command is written. Be sure to USE the newly sorted file to view the results.

7. Quit or continue

EXERCISE 4.6. HOW TO GET THE MOST FROM dBASE COMMANDS

The commands discussed in this lesson will continue to use the COMMAND mode as reference. They are useful commands to use when accessing the data of any file.

The LIST Command

The LIST command has been discussed; however, other options are available to you when using LIST. As with the DISPLAY command, LIST may be used to show selected records of a file.

With the CUSTOMER file active,

1. At the dot prompt, type **.LIST NAME**

2. Press **Enter**

   Only the names are displayed. You may use this command to list any field name.

3. Type **.LIST NAME,CUSTNUM**

4. Press **Enter** (pressing Enter after typing in entry will be assumed through the remainder of the instructions)

   Notice that this time the location of CUSTNUM moved so that it now follows the NAME field. You can list the fields in any order and thus view them differently from the original order.

5. Type **.LIST RECORD 8**

   The command allows you to view the single Record 8.

The SKIP Command

This command will advance the pointer forward one record. You can enter either a positive number to move forward in the file or a negative number to move backwards in the file.

1. Type

   .LIST RECORD 9
   .SKIP

   A message saying Record No. 10 is showing.

2. Type **.DISPLAY** to display Record 10.

3. Type **.SKIP -5** (use the minus sign) to move to Record 5

4. Type **.DISPLAY** to view Record 5

The GOTO TOP and GOTO BOTTOM Commands

These commands do just what they sound like they would do. They go to the first or last record in the file.

1. Type

   .GOTO TOP
   .DISPLAY

   The first record is shown.

2. Type

   .GOTO BOTTOM
   .DISPLAY

   The last record is shown (Number 16).

The REPLACE Command

You can use the REPLACE command to quickly replace the contents of certain cells throughout a file. This command will replace one value or label in a field for another.

An example: Suppose you want to replace the charge, F, with a T for customer Wayne Montoya. You would simply,

1. Type

   .REPLACE CHARGE WITH .T. FOR NAME='Wayne Montoya'

The message "1 record replaced" appears.

2. List the records or just Record 8 to see the change in Montoya's Charge field.

The LOCATE Command

This command will search for an occurrence in the field, and once found, will list the record number of the occurrence.

1. Type **.LOCATE FOR CITY="BOULDER"**

   The statement "Record=1" appears.

2. Type **.CONTINUE**

   to continue to the next occurrence (Record = 6).

   When you locate an occurrence, you may, of course, display the record contents.

3. Keep typing **.CONTINUE** at the dot prompts until all occurrences are found and the message

   "END of LOCATE scope" appears.

The SEEK Command

The SEEK command is used with any file containing an index. Both the main file and the index must be referenced in a USE statement prior to issuing the SEEK command. The index is used to find records during a SEEK process. Start a SEEK process with the CUSTOMER file and its ZIPINDEX file:

1. Type

   .USE CUSTOMER INDEX ZIPINDEX

NOTE: Any index file could be used.

2. Type **.SEEK '80302'**

   The first occurrence of zip code 80302 is located.

3. To see the record, type **.DISPLAY**

   Using the SKIP command and DISPLAY again will show the next occurrence of the 80302 zip. You must continue this process until a zip other than 80302 is located.

4. Quit. Complete the review questions and then continue to the next lesson.

Review Questions for Exercises 4.4, 4.5, and 4.6

1. What is the DISPLAY command used to turn the record numbers off?

2. Write a DISPLAY statement that will list the fields, NAME, ADDRESS, ZIP of a current database file.

3. Write a DISPLAY statement that will list all records for those persons with a zip code of 98026 when the field is called ZIP.

4. Write a DISPLAY statement for all persons whose NAME is Smith and whose ZIP is 98112.

5. What is the command for tallying all records in a database field?

6. What is the command used to sum a numeric field?

7. How is a field averaged?

8. What is the command to create an index on the NAME field to a new index (create your own index name) file?

9. What is the command used to SORT on the ZIP field to a new file (create your own filename for the sorted file)?

10. How do you view a sorted file?

11. How do you list specific fields in a file?

12. What is the command used to move quickly to the first or last record in a file?

13. What is the command used to quickly replace all Ts (for True) in a logical field throughout an entire database?

14. How do you locate the first record having a ZIP of 98027?

15. What does the SEEK command do? What command follows the SEEK command in order to see the results of your SEEK?

Answers to the Review Questions on Exercises 4.4, 4.5, and 4.6

1. .DISPLAY ALL OFF
2. .DISPLAY ALL NAME, ADDRESS, ZIP
3. .DISPLAY ALL FOR ZIP = 98026
4. .DISPLAY ALL FOR NAME = "SMITH" .AND. ZIP = 98112
5. .COUNT
6. .SUM COST
   Where COST is a numeric field.
7. .AVERAGE COST
8. .INDEX ON NAME TO NAMEINDX
9. .SORT ON ZIP TO CUSTZIP
   Where CUSTOMER is the main database file.
10. .USE CUSTZIP
    .LIST
11. .LIST NAME, ADDRESS, ZIP
12. .GOTO TOP
    .GOTO BOTTOM
13. .REPLACE MEMBER WITH .F. FOR ZIP=98027
    Where MEMBER is the name of the field containing the T and all zip code areas of 98027 will change to F (for false) in the MEMBER field.
14. .LOCATE FOR ZIP="98027"
15. It locates a particular data item, such as 98027 in the ZIP field or Smith in the NAME field.
    .DISPLAY

ADVANCED DATABASE FUNCTIONS

EXERCISE 4.7. HOW TO CREATE A REPORT

One of the most useful features of dBASE is its report-generation capability. In this section you will create the report shown in Figure 4-12. It uses the information from the file you created earlier, SALES.

02/10/90

January Sales

Vendor	Description	Quantity Sold	Price	Amount
** Funk				
Funk	Indy Jones Jacket, large	30	90.00	2700.00
Funk	Rozelle Headband	10	6.00	60.00
** Subtotal **		40		2760.00
** Peak				
Peak	Nordic Hat	85	10.00	850.00
Peak	Nylon Windpants	50	40.00	2000.00
Peak	Thermal Ski Socks	100	7.00	700.00
** Subtotal **		235		3550.00
*** Total ***		275		6310.00

Figure 4-12. dBASE III PLUS Report

The report shown above has two interesting characteristics that you commonly find in business reports. One characteristic is the calculated field. Notice that the last column of the report, "Amount," is not a field in the SALES file. It was created from two fields of this file—QUANTITY and PRICE. The second feature is the use of control breaks. Notice that after each supplier—Funk Fashions (Funk) and Peak Mountaineering (Peak)—dBASE breaks to print a subtotal of the Quantity Sold and Amount columns. Also, at the end of the report, there is a final break taken to print totals. In dBASE, and in other report generators, you can specify which fields you want to use to control the breaks in the report (the SUPPLIER field in Figure 4-12) and which columns you want totaled.

Preparing a dBASE report involves three steps:

1. Establishing a source data file or environment: The file containing the source data for the report will generally be an ordinary .DBF file. You have already created this file and called it SALES. If you decide, you may sort the file prior to creating the report. In order to run subtotals as in the report shown in Figure 4-12, you must sort the field name whose groups of values you wish to subtotal; for example, sort Supplier to see the subtotals for each.

2. Defining the report format: This step is the most important step in creating a report. It is the step in which you tell dBASE what the report will look like, how it will be titled, what fields will be calculated or used for control breaks, and so forth. dBASE uses a separate file to store all of this information about how the report will be prepared. This file is called a report form and has the extension of .FRM.

3. Outputting the report: In this step you point dBASE to the report form that you want to output and instruct dBASE to display the report or to send the report to the printer.

To Prepare the Report

You have already created the data file that will be used in this exercise.

1. Make the SALES file active through the USE command from the COMMAND mode

The SALES file is the source file whose data will be used to create the report. It is now time to define your report.

2. Sort the file on the SUPPLIER column to a file called SALESSUP

3. Make SALESSUP the active file (.USE SALESSUP)

In ASSIST:

4. Choose Report from the Create menu

5. Select B: (or A: for a hard disk system) from the disk-drive submenu that appears and then

To respond to the filename prompt,

6. Type **SALESR**

7. Press **Enter**

NOTE: SALESR will be the name of the report. It will appear on the disk and in the directory as SALESR.FRM

The menu in Figure 4-13 appears.

Options | Groups | Columns | Locate | Exit | 07:15:10 pm

Page title	
Page width (positions)	80
Left margin	8
Right margin	0
Lines per page	58
Double space rept	No
Page eject before printing	Yes
Page eject after printing	No
Plain page	No

CURSOR <-- -->	Delete char: Del	Insert column: ^N	Insert: Ins
Char: <- ->	Delete word: ^T	Report format: F1	Zoom in: ^PgDn
Word: Home End	Delete column: ^U	Abandon: Esc	Zoom out: ^PgUp

CREATE REPORT <A:> B:SALESR.FRM Option 1/9

Position selection bar - | | . Select - ↵ Leave menu - <- ->

Enter up to four lines of text to be displayed at the top of each report page.

Figure 4-13. Opening Report Screen

The menu bar at the top of the screen contains report-generation commands that you will use to prepare various parts of the report. The drop down box under the Options menu contains a list of the default settings for the output of the report. It shows the standard page width, the left margin and right margin spaces, as well as the lines per page. Usually these default settings are correct as they stand; however, you may adjust the settings if you want to change the appearance of your final report. For this exercise, leave them as they are.

8. Press **Enter** to select the Page title option

The following box appears next to the Options box.

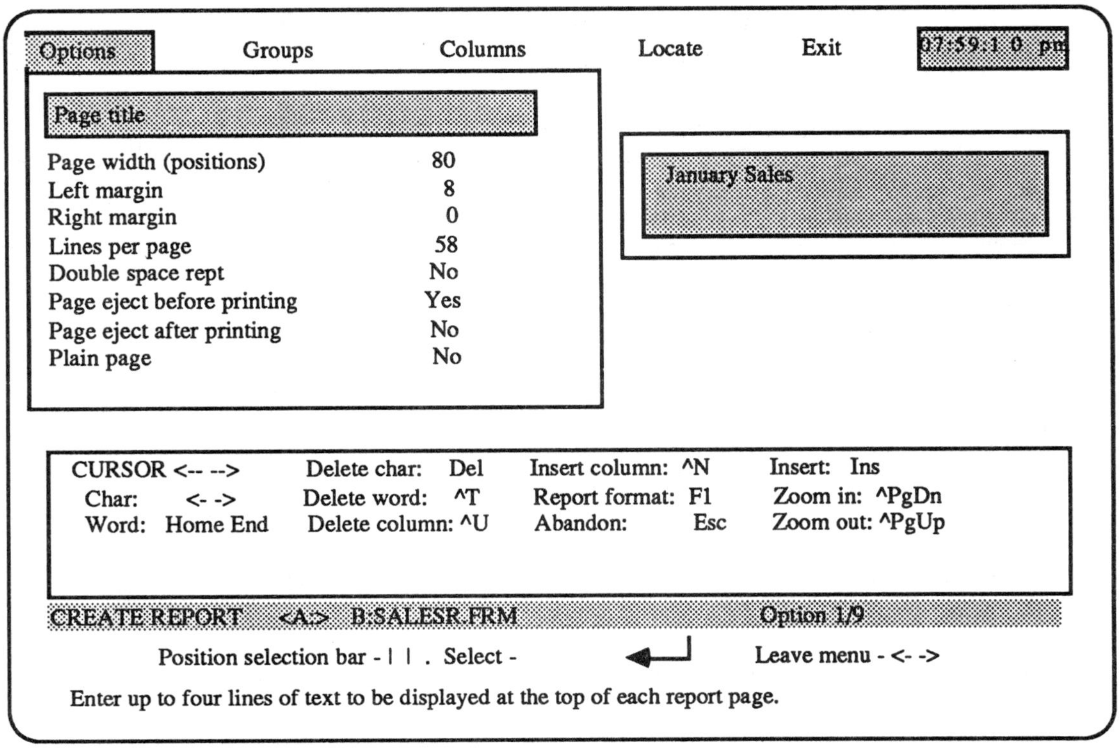

Figure 4-14. Giving the Report a Title

This box allows you to enter a title of up to four lines for the main heading of the report.

9. Type **January Sales** and press **Enter**

As with other means of exiting and saving an entry, you can see that Ctrl End will save the report title and exit you from this particular command mode.

10. Press **^End** (Ctrl End)

11. Press the **Right Arrow** key once to move to the Groups menu

A screen similar to the one in Figure 4-15 appears.

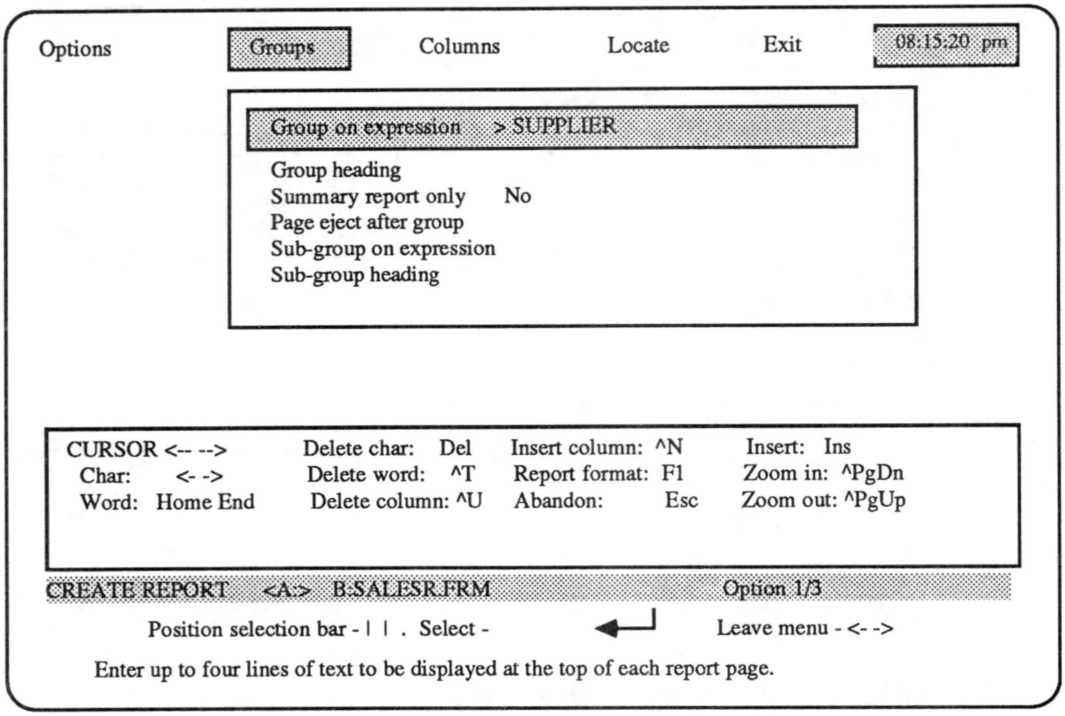

Figure 4-15. Identifying the Field by Which to Group

From this menu you can identify the field that will serve as the control field. The control field designates where subtotals will appear in the final report. It tells the program that each division under the field name SUPPLIER will show a subtotal.

12. Press **Enter** to select the Group on expression option

A small arrow appears to the right of the expression. The arrow designates where you can begin entering information AND tells you that you are READY to enter information. Without the presence of the arrow, you would not be allowed to type the information.

13. Type **SUPPLIER** (in CAPS exactly as you entered the field name)

NOTE: You could also press F10 to see a list of your field names. You would then highlight the correct field name and press Enter.

14. Press **Enter**

The arrow disappears.

15. Press the **Right Arrow** again, one time, to move to the Columns menu.

A menu similar to the one shown in Figure 4-16 appears.

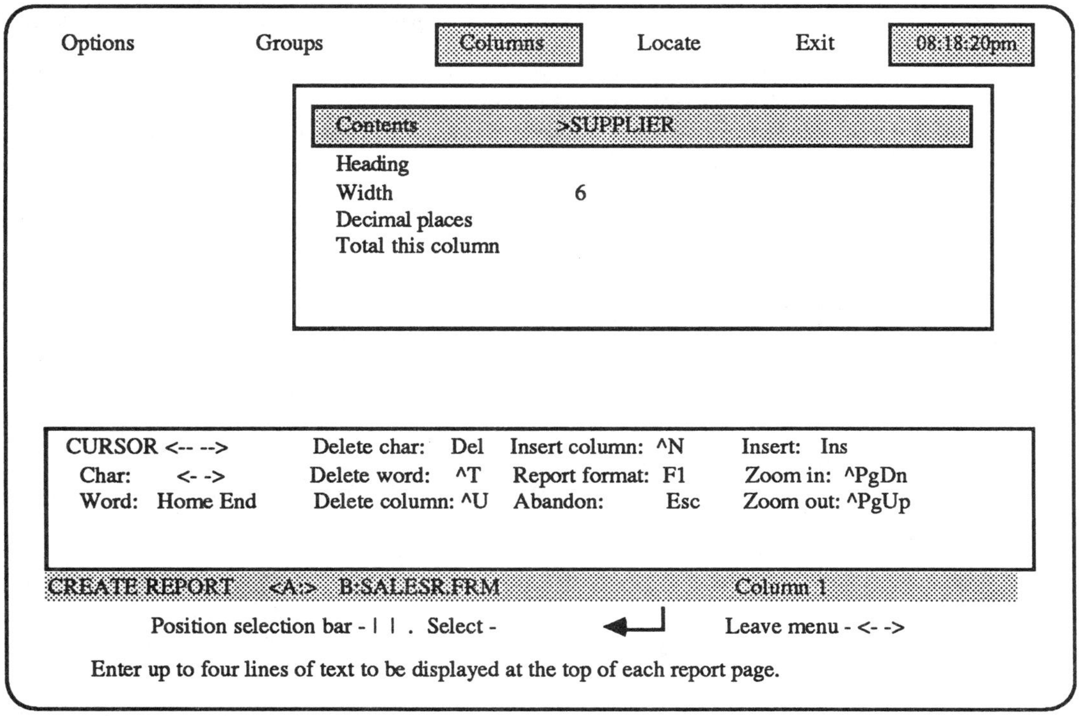

Figure 4-16. Creating the First Report Column

From this menu, you will explain to dBASE what the columns of the report will contain. Look once again at the columns in Figure 4-12. They are:

Vendor
Description
Quantity Sold
Price
Amount

A total of five columns needs to be defined for this report.

16. Press **Enter** to select the first command in this menu, Contents

NOTE: Once again the arrow appears indicating that you are ready to type the contents for this column.

Type the contents of the first column. The contents will be from one of the fields in the database file SALES. In this case the contents will be from the field SUPPLIER.

17. Type **SUPPLIER** (or press **F10** to highlight SUPPLIER from a list) and press **Enter**

18. Use the **Down Arrow** Key to move to the next option, Heading.

NOTE: At the bottom of your screen is a list of the commands to give to move up and down in the menu, to select an option on the menu, and to leave the menu. Use the up and down arrows, the Enter key, and the left and right arrows, respectively, to move through and out of any of the menus.

19. Define the remainder of the SUPPLIER column as follows:

    a. For Heading, type **Vendor** and press **CtrlEnd**

    "Vendor" is the title that will appear above the first column.

    b. Press the **Down Arrow** to the width setting. For Width, type **6**.

    This is the maximum width of the field when it prints.

    c. For Decimal places, you can leave this item blank

    This is only applicable in numeric fields; used to set the places to the right of the decimal.

    d. For Total this column, leave blank

    When the field is numeric, the total will automatically be inserted.

NOTE: Use the Enter key after typing the headings or other information; use the Down Arrow to move to the next field in the column; use PgDn to finish the column and begin identifying the next column.

As you are entering the remaining information in Figure 4-17, watch the bottom of the screen. A sample report format shows exactly what the layout of your report will look like when printed. The XXXXs represent the width of the column in character format; the #####s represent the width of a numeric column and the ####.##s, with a decimal, represent the width of a column using decimals.

PgUp will move you back in your fields if you want to make a change in the layout.

20. Set the remainder of the columns as shown in Figure 4-17.

Contents field	Headings field	Width field	Total-this-column field
SUPPLIER	Vendor	6	---
DESCRIP	bbbbDescription	25	---
QUANTITY	bQuantity bbSold	8	Yes
PRICE	bbPrice	8	No
QUANTITY*PRICE	bbbAmount	10	Yes

b=leading blank space

Figure 4-17. Data Specified under "Columns" Option on Report Menu Bar

When finished with the description of the report layout,

21. Press the **Right Arrow** key twice to the Exit menu

22. Press **Enter** on the Save option

The report form is saved, and you return to the ASSIST mode.

To Output the Report

1. Choose the Report option on the Retrieve menu on the ASSIST mode

2. Choose the B: (or A: for a hard disk system) drive from the disk-drive submenu

3. Choose SALESR.FRM from the submenu that appears

4. Choose Execute the command

5. To send the output to both the printer and the display screen, press **Y** to respond to the prompt asking "Direct output to the printer?"

PRACTICE DOCUMENTS

PRACTICE DOCUMENT 1: EMPLOYEE DONATIONS RECORD

Objectives:

In this exercise, you will practice

a. creating a database file
b. using both the ASSIST mode and the COMMAND mode
c. defining data
d. listing records
e. leaving and entering the database
f. viewing the directory
g. setting the default drive
h. using a stored file
i. appending records
j. printing a file

1. Create a database file called DOC3 for the records shown below. Count the maximum number of characters used in each column to decide on the width of the fields. Define Salary as numeric; define all other fields as character fields.

   The fields are:

   EMPLOYEE
   TELEPHONE
   GENDER
   EMPLOYED
   SALARY
   DONATION

   The employees are:

   Pratt, John
   225-1234
   M
   06/22/88
   1949.00
   200.00

   Jones, David
   292-3832
   M
   06/15/88
   1500.00
   225.00

Smoller, Ellen
225-3212
F
09/15/88
1650.00
300.00

Sill, Sally
224-4321
F
02/15/87
1800.00
150.00

Knat, Michael
221-1235
M
09/15/80
1700.00
350.00

Smith, Paul
223-8251
M
11/01/85
1800.00
200.50

2. After defining the fields, exit without entering data

3. Append the file to enter data

4. Exit from the program

5. Sign on to the program

6. Set the default drive

7. View the directory to be sure DOC3 is listed

8. Open the database file, DOC3

9. List the file to be sure it is accurate

10. Append the database to add the following three records

Martins, Mary
222-2123
F
11/01/85
1850.00
175.00

Beam, Sandy
225-6912
F
02/15/86
1450.00
275.00

Johnson, Frank
223-7928
M
03/20/86
1500.00
0.00

11. Print a copy of the database records

PRACTICE DOCUMENT 2: PAYROLL REPORT

Objectives:

In this exercise, you will practice

a. creating a database
b. defining the fields in a database
c. using the APPEND command
d. deleting and recalling records
e. sorting data
f. listing specific records and fields
g. using the DISPLAY command
h. using the EDIT and BROWSE commands

1. Create a database file called DOC4. It will contain the following fields:

   ID NUMBER
   EMPLOYEE NAME
   DEPARTMENT
   PAY RATE
   GROSS PAY

2. Immediately after defining the fields, enter the data as shown below:

   278
   Ronald H. Dougherty
   MIS
   12.50
   500.00

   178
   James Jordan
   Payroll
   15.50
   620.00

   292
   Bonnie J. Smith
   Customer Services
   13.40
   536.00

   346
   Cynthia Clement
   MIS
   18.90
   756.00

415
Helen Zonguldake
Personnel
12.00
480.00

595
Donald Foster, Sr.
MIS
22.00
880.00

150
Charles VanderZee
Personnel
20.00
800.00

420
Helen Aiken
Payroll
17.50
700.00

3. Sort the file in ascending order

4. Print a copy of the file

5. Use the BROWSE command to change the following:

   a. Ronald Dougherty's salary to $13.00 (adjust the total by multiplying by 40 and make correction)
   b. Bonnie Smith's department to Personnel
   c. Helen Zonguldake's department to Customer Services

6. Use the LIST command to show all persons working in the MIS department. Show the names and departments only.

7. Use the DISPLAY command to show the following:

   a. the names of all persons in Payroll
   b. a list of all persons earning more than $12.00 an hour
   c. the names of all persons who are either working in MIS or making less than $20.00 an hour

8. Mark Record 4 for deletion. List the file to be sure it is marked. Recall the record. List the file again to be sure the record is no longer marked.

9. Sort the file by Name in ascending order and by Department in descending order. Print a copy of the sorted file.

10. Use the LIST command to show Record 3

11. Use the EDIT command to edit Record 3. Make the following changes:

    a. add a J. as the middle initial
    b. change the hourly wage to 24.00
    c. adjust the weekly wage

12. Display the file to the printer

PRACTICE DOCUMENT 3: SOFTWARE SALES SHEET

Objectives:

In this exercise, you will practice:

a. creating a database
b. modifying the database
c. creating an index
d. sorting the file using the SET command
e. creating a report

1. Create a database file called DOC5 for the following table:

SOFTWARE SALES

CUSTNUM	ITEM	DATE SOLD	PRICE	QUANTITY	TOTAL
1232	Database Text	01/10/90	200.00	1	200.00
2388	Database Text	01/10/90	200.00	1	200.00
3445	Database Tutor	01/08/90	70.00	1	70.00
3442	Database Tutor	01/08/90	70.00	1	70.00
1232	Graphics	01/09/90	200.00	2	400.00
6224	Database Tutor	01/09/90	70.00	1	70.00
1232	Reports Pkg	01/09/90	150.00	1	150.00
1332	Spreadsheet	01/09/90	150.00	3	450.00
2445	Spreadsheet	01/11/90	150.00	1	150.00
2443	Time Mgt	01/09/90	300.00	2	600.00
6223	Time Mgt	01/10/90	300.00	3	900.00
3445	Database Text	01/11/90	200.00	3	600.00
5122	Database Text	01/11/90	200.00	5	1000.00
5223	Database Text	01/11/90	200.00	3	600.00
5432	Database Text	02/10/90	200.00	1	200.00
6223	Graphics	01/20/90	200.00	5	1000.00
2883	Reports Pkg	02/10/90	150.00	2	300.00
2443	Reports Pkg	02/05/90	150.00	3	450.00

2. Create an index with the key field of CUSTNUM to an index file called NUMINDX

3. Use the SET command to sort the records

4. List the records after the SET command. A listing of the records sorting on the field CUSTNUM will appear.

5. Create a report, using the following instructions:

   a. Specify the main heading as:

SOFTWARE MANUAL SALES
JANUARY 10 THROUGH FEBRUARY 10, 1990

b. Create the following column headings:

Customer Number
Item Sold
Date Sold
Unit Price
Quantity Sold
Total Sale

c. Divide the report into item description subcategories and subtotal each group

6. Output the report to the printer

COMMAND SUMMARY

As with the other Command Summaries in this guide, this one should be used for reference ONLY after having completed all exercises in this section. In this summary, fieldnames and file-names used in examples are shown in < >. Where the steps from the COMMAND mode were considered most efficient, they are the only ones listed in response to the procedure to use.

Adding Records

1. Type **.APPEND**

Adding Values in Fields

examples:

.SUM PRICE

.SUM QUANTITY

To add fields with specific conditions:

.SUM PRICE FOR SUPPLIER = "SeaTech Corp."

Averaging Fields

examples:

.AVERAGE PRICE

.AVERAGE QUANTITY

Assist Mode (Moving To It)

When in COMMAND mode:

Press **F2** or type **ASSIST** at the dot prompt

Command Mode (Moving To It)

When in the ASSIST mode:

Press **Esc**

Creating a Database

In ASSIST:

1. Choose Database from the Create menu
2. Choose the drive on which you want to save the file
3. Type the filename

Creating Reports

With the database active:

Type **.CREATE REPORT** <report name>

In COMMAND mode:

Type **.CREATE** <filename>

Default Drive (Setting)

In ASSIST:

Type **.SET DEFAULT TO B:** (or **A:** for hard disk systems)

Displaying a Report on the Screen

Type **.REPORT FORM** <report name>

Exiting the Program

Type **.QUIT**

Field Descriptors

To move from field to field:

Press **Enter**

To change the type of field:

Press the **spacebar**

Help

Press **F1**

Modifying Reports

With the database active:

Type **.MODIFY REPORT** <report name>

Modifying a Database File

In ASSIST:

Choose Database from the Modify menu

Opening an Existing File

Type **.USE** <filename>

Deleting Rocords

This command marks the record with an asterisk.

To delete a single record:

Type **.DELETE RECORD** <#>

Example: .DELETE RECORD 2

To delete records containing a like condition:

.DELETE FOR STATE = "CO"
.DELETE FOR CHARGE = ".F."

Recalling a Deleted Record

This command recalls records marked with an asterisk through the DELETE command.

Type **.RECALL RECORD** <#>

Example: .RECALL RECORD 2

Deleting a Record Permanently

Use this command after records are marked with an asterisk (*), using the DELETE command.

Type **.PACK**

Editing Records

With the BROWSE command:

1. Type **.BROWSE**

2. Press **PgUp** to see all records

With the EDIT command:

.EDIT RECORD <#>

Example: .EDIT RECORD 2

Example 2: .EDIT FOR STATE = "WA"

Counting Records

Counting all records:

Type **.COUNT**

Counting for specific conditions:

Type **.COUNT FOR STATE = "WA"**

Indexing Records

Type **.SORT ON** <field name> to <new index name>

To view the indexed file:

Type **.SET INDEX TO** <new index name>

Listing Records

Listing all records of the active file:

Type **.LIST**

Listing some fields:

Type **.LIST NAME, ADDRESS**

Listing a record:

Type **.LIST RECORD 8**

Moving through a File

To the top of a file:

Type **.GOTO TOP**
.DISPLAY

To the bottom of a file:

Type **.GOTO BOTTOM**
.DISPLAY

Printing a Report

Type **.REPORT FORM** <report name> **TO PRINT**

Replacing Data in Records

Type **.REPLACE** <field name> **WITH** <new data> **FOR** <field name>=<condition>

Example:

.REPLACE STATUS WITH .Y. FOR NAME="Sam Jones"

Searching Records

To locate the first occurrence in a file:

Type **.LOCATE FOR CITY = "SEATTLE"**

To locate the next occurrence of the above command:

Type **.CONTINUE**

With this command, keep typing CONTINUE at the dot prompt until all occurrences of SEATTLE are found (or any other condition) at which time the message, END of LOCATE, will appear.

With the SEEK command:

The SEEK command may be used to search records ONLY when the file has been indexed.

Example:

1. Use the index created
2. Type **.USE CUSTOMER INDEX ZIPINDEX**
3. (an index that was created called ZIPINDEX from the CUSTOMER file)
4. Type **.DISPLAY**

Signing on to the Program

With a hard disk system:

1. Change to the dBASE directory
2. At the dBASE prompt, type **dBASE** (in upper or lower case)

With a dual-disk system:

1. Insert the System 1 disk in Drive A
2. Insert the data disk in Drive B
3. Type **dBASE** at the A>
4. Press **Enter**
5. Follow the screen messages and insert the System 2 disk in Drive A when prompted to do so
6. Press **Enter**

Sorting Records

Type **.SORT ON** <fieldname> **TO** <new sorted filename>

To view the sorted file:

Type **.USE** <new sorted filename>

Viewing All .DBF Files

.DIR

Viewing All Files on any Directory

In ASSIST:

1. Press **T** for Tools
2. Directory
3. Press **Enter**
4. Choose Drive
5. Press **Enter**
6. Highlight file extensions to list
7. Press **Enter**

Viewing All Records

Type **.LIST**

Viewing All Records a Screen at a Time

Type **.DISPLAY ALL**

Other examples:

To show all records without the record numbers:

Type **.DISPLAY ALL OFF**

To display specific fields:

Type **.DISPLAY ALL OFF** <field1>,<field2>,<field3>

To display for a specific condition:

Type **.DISPLAY ALL OFF FOR STATE ="WA"**

To display for two conditions:

Type **.DISPLAY ALL OFF FOR STATE = "WA" .AND. ZIP = "98122"**

To display for one condition or another condition:

Type **.DISPLAY ALL OFF FOR STATE = "WA" .OR. STATE = "CO"**

NOTES

INDEX

School Software Direct Order Form

☐ Ship to student ☐ Ship to reseller (replacement stock)

Qualifying teachers, as well as college, university, and other post-secondary students, can now purchase WordPerfect Corporation (WPCORP) software directly from WPCORP at a reduced price. To qualify, a participant must be a full-time teacher/administrator or currently enrolled as a full-time post-secondary student, and must agree in writing not to resell or transfer any package purchased under this program.

If you satisfy these qualifying conditions and would like to purchase software directly from WPCORP under the School Software Program, complete the following six steps and sign at the bottom of the form.

Step 1. From the list below, select the appropriate software and disk size for your computer (please note that you are limited to *one* package of each program) and mark an "x" in the corresponding box(es).

Product	Price*	Disk Size
☐ WordPerfect 5.0—IBM Personal Computers	$135.00	☐ 3½" ☐ 5¼"
☐ WordPerfect 4.2—IBM PC & Compatibles	125.00	☐ 3½" ☐ 5¼"
☐ WordPerfect—Apple IIe/IIc	59.00	☐ 3½" & 5¼"
☐ WordPerfect—Apple IIGS	59.00	☐ 3½"
☐ WordPerfect—Amiga	99.00	☐ 3½"
☐ WordPerfect—Atari ST	99.00	☐ 3½"
☐ WordPerfect—Macintosh	99.00	☐ 3½"
☐ PlanPerfect—IBM PC & Compatibles	99.00	☐ 3½" ☐ 5¼"
☐ DataPerfect—IBM PC & Compatibles	150.00	☐ 3½" & 5¼"
☐ WordPerfect Library—IBM PC & Compatibles	59.00	☐ 3½" & 5¼"
☐ WordPerfect Library—Amiga	59.00	☐ 3½"
☐ WordPerfect Executive—IBM PC & Compatibles	79.00	☐ 3½" & 5¼"
☐ Junior WordPerfect—IBM PC & Compatibles	35.00	☐ 5¼"
☐ WordPerfect, Foreign Versions—IBM PC & Compatibles Language ________	175.00	☐ 3½" ☐ 5¼"
☐ WordPerfect Speller, Foreign Versions—IBM PC & Compatibles Language ________	40.00	☐ 3½" ☐ 5¼"

**No changes or additions can be made to this list.*

Step 2. Make a photocopy of your current Student ID or Faculty card *and* a photocopy of some well known form of identification displaying your social security number, such as your Driver License or Social Security Card. (WPCORP will hold this information strictly confidential and use it only to guard against duplicate purchases.) Your school ID must show current enrollment. (If it does not show a date, you must send verification of current enrollment.) If you have serious reservations about providing a social security number, call the Education Division at (801) 227-7131 to establish clearance to purchase any of the above software products at these special prices.

Step 3. Enter your social security number: __ __ __ – __ __ – __ __ __ __ .

Step 4. Enclose payment for the total cost of the package(s) ordered with personal check, money order, Visa, or MasterCard.

Account # ____________________ Expiration Date ________ ☐ VISA ☐ MasterCard

(Make check or money order payable to WordPerfect Corporation.)

Step 5. List your shipping address and the address of your local computer store (dealer) in the space provided:

Ship To ____________________ Designated Dealer ____________________

____________________ ____________________

____________________ ____________________

Phone ____________________ Phone ____________________

Step 6. Enclose this signed and completed form, the photocopies of your identification cards, and your signed check or money order (or Visa or MasterCard account number and expiration date) in an envelope and mail to School Software Program, WordPerfect Corporation, 1555 N. Technology Way, Orem, UT 84057.

The information provided herein is correct and accurate, and I will abide by the restricting conditions outlined by WPCORP in this document. I understand that at its sole discretion, WPCORP may refuse any order for any reason.

Signature ____________________ Date ____________________

*Utah residents add 6.25% sales tax. Prices are quoted in U.S. dollars and apply to U.S. delivery for U.S. customers *only*.

WordPerfect Corporation • 1555 N. Technology Way • Orem, Utah 84057 • (801) 225-5000